A SEASON IN HELL

A SEASON
IN HELL

☆

THE LIFE OF
ARTHUR RIMBAUD

BY

JEAN-MARIE CARRE

☆

TRANSLATED BY
HANNAH AND MATTHEW JOSEPHSON

☆

M. EVANS
Lanham • New York • Boulder • Toronto • Plymouth, UK

M. Evans
An imprint of The Rowman & Littlefield Publishing Group, Inc.
4501 Forbes Boulevard, Suite 200, Lanham, Maryland 20706
http://www.rlpgtrade.com

10 Thornbury Road, Plymouth PL6 7PP, United Kingdom

Distributed by National Book Network

Library of Congress Cataloging-in-Publication Data Available

ISBN 13: 978-1-59077-485-4 (pbk: alk. paper)

♾™ The paper used in this publication meets the minimum requirements of American National Standard for Information Sciences—Permanence of Paper for Printed Library Materials, ANSI/NISO Z39.48-1992.

Printed in the United States of America

TRANSLATOR'S NOTE

Specimens of Rimbaud's work have been added as an appendix to this biography, thanks to the interest and the co-operation of a number of writers who have made translations at various times and given permission for their use here. A great debt is owing to Dr. James Sibley Watson, for his translation of the *Season in Hell*, originally published in *The Dial*, 1920, and reprinted here. The version is a faithful one; the apparent excesses of rhetoric are no more startling than in the original French of Rimbaud's farewell to literature. Almost as much of Rimbaud's character may be gathered from a study of *The Drunken Boat*, which has received a most remarkable rendering into English verse by Mr. Lionel Abel, who has permitted the publication of his work here. Our gratitude is also due to Mr. Joseph T. Shipley and Mr. T. Sturge Moore, for their excellent English versions of a poet who has been long considered untranslatable.

CONTENTS

CONTENTS

Part III—Defeated

Appendix

FOUR POEMS, BY ARTHUR RIMBAUD

INTRODUCTION

The "revival" of Jean-Arthur Rimbaud, and the modern cult of him as a poet and an oracle, has all the air of one of those celebrated cases which, like the rescue of Blake or Melville from Limbo, periodically dislocate the history of letters. After fifty years of the Rimbaud legend—it has flourished more magnificently than ever in the post-war decade—new aspects of interest emerge for us continually, as scholars piece together, like some beautiful ruined statuary, his singular history.

The present biography by J-M. Carré, a native of the Ardennes, Rimbaud's country, is a work of sincere scholarship whose purpose is primarily historical. Greatly admiring Rimbaud, M. Carré seems to have been the least mystical, the least partial, the least given to suspicion and conjecture, among the several historians of the "lost poet." He has been most comprehensive in the use of all the real documents; and the present translation has been augmented over the original edition of Paris, 1926, by various notes upon new manuscripts or letters

9

lately discovered. Where acrid controversy has raged for a generation over Rimbaud, so that one view holds him damned, or an evil genius, while the other holds him one of the chosen souls, it is no small triumph to have been impartial. His Excellency, M. Paul Claudel, for instance, regards the poet as a Catholic mystic "in the *wild state*, a lost spring reissuing from a saturated soil"; he ascribes his own religious conversion to Rimbaud's example! And when we consider that the intransigeantly modern *Surrealistes* also take Rimbaud to be their apostle, then we may gauge how extremely wide are the ramifications of his influence. Angel or demon?—M. Carré believes him to be both, "that is, human, even to a superhuman degree."

Genius of poetry though he undoubtedly was, the most beautiful and enigmatic thing of all Rimbaud did was certainly his own life. It has the aspects of profound interior drama and extravagant physical adventure. He was precocious; for two or three years, after the age of sixteen, he wrote verses and prose stamped with greatness. Yet at nineteen he abandoned literature for good and all; he also put behind him completely European civilization itself, to embark upon fabulous adventures in the Orient and lose himself in its more primitive life-currents. That he was fully aware of all his own powers and of the meaning of every step he took—such as the attempted destruction of his manuscripts—makes his case all the more haunting. His life has a dreadful beauty. Because he "struggled in vain to escape a Voice that solicited him," as Claudel says? Or is it as some "terrible messenger," as a figure of absolute revolt against the culture of the Western world that he troubles and looms over us?

His own sparse writings, little known during his violent and brief artistic career, and which M. Carré treats of indirectly in tracing the life, seem to prophesy and record his personal fate. Beyond the immediate brilliance of device and literary effect, his work has the refulgence of his strange destiny as a seeker of the "primitive," as a kind of superman— so the French have always believed—contemporary to the still unknown Nietzsche. The fantastic and sonorous lines of *The Drunken Boat*, the spiritual drama of a Lucifer in his *Season in Hell* (1873), which he called his "Nigger book," his last testament to posterity—all this is a consistent and inconceivably bitter repudiation of his age, an age outwardly mercenary and spiritually defeated; and all of it exercises a perpetual invitation to uneasy little men of letters or men of the world to abandon their hollow arts and advance with Rimbaud into the unknown, the nameless, and the vertiginous.

Yet his writings, which he himself spurned, seem also to beckon one back, reviving, illuminating, as one disciple declares, "all the ways of art, of religion and life." There are even interpreters who have identified an "expansive" mystical religion, like the faith of the Upanishads and the Bhagavad-Gita, in Rimbaud's flight from the real and in the outcries, the cabbalistic fragments of the *Season in*

11

Hell. One feels incompetent to follow these obscure intimations. But what is clear is that there was expressed in Rimbaud at one stage, a religion of art, a religion of pure literature. He himself, after long and fearful vigils, was to learn something that made him curse art and flee it; but he left certain secrets or clues which men seized upon, under the overwhelming temptation to become alchemists in their turn.

*　*　*

Paul Valéry, in writing on the French "Symbolists" of the late nineteenth century, speaks of the high aspirations of this literary school, of its painful search for pure forms, determined by musical unity, and even for a kind of "universal language of ideas," presented through images or symbols. But, he concludes, a too rarefied zone had been reached, an air "too pure" and unbreathable, from which retreat was inevitable. Had not Rimbaud foreseen all this? He was of course the precursor of all the modern literary movements which have been variously called "symbolist" or "abstract" or "experimental." Elsewhere Valéry observes: "We have all been feeding upon Rimbaud, these forty years."

The modern literary movements are indeed all directly traceable to Poe, who in the *Eureka* seemed to be groping toward the realization of a "universal symmetry" present in his mind, through his "poetic instinct." His literature, instead of being merely "representative" was peopled with the figures or the symbols of his imagination. Now Baudelaire, who

12

felt that Poe had anticipated all of his ideas, became his inspired translator; Baudelaire in turn, by poems and translations, had a decisive effect upon Rimbaud. So that when young American poets, exposed to French literature, now absorb Rimbaud's influence directly, or even at second or third hand, they still remain within the orbit of an American tradition.

The character of Rimbaud bears many points of resemblance to that of the elder American. He borrowed freely from various sources, from Racine, Hugo, and Baudelaire; and yet like the other, he was a supremely inventive spirit. Paul Verlaine, his pathetic companion and protector during his Bohemian days, thought Rimbaud possessed; he believed that his youthful friend was a magician and a Seer who "knew all commerce, art, medicine"; who could possibly "re-invent life." And indeed the sixteen-year-old seemed full of sorcery; he was naturally a wonder-worker, though of few productions. He had the endowments of the poet: a sensorium capable of immense vibrations, the eye "in frenzy rolling," the lordly language; he had an instinctive command of his craft, so that his deliberately conceived effects, now of bursts of color, or light, quick movements, or sonority, seem to be achieved with a certain and easy stroke.

An early letter of 1871, called the "letter of the Seer," reveals his theories and plans which were soon to be fulfilled in the poem of *The Drunken Boat* and in the *Illuminations*. He speaks to his friend of his

13

scorn for the contemporary literary schools, mediocre second generation of romantics. The poet must refuse the way of compromise and imitation; casting off his false education, he must turn barbarous, become again "the Stealer of Fire."

"*Je est un autre*," he writes; which may be translated: "The *I* is another self." One part of the poet, the *I*, gives himself up to the vigilant study of the other self. "He searches for his soul, inspects it, tests it, knows it." He is present at "the unfolding of his own thought"; hangs upon it, poised; gives a stroke of his baton, and lo, the full orchestra sounds for him. But this mastery, this "cultivation of the self," must become something dangerous. He says: "*It is a question of making the soul monstrous in the manner of the comprachicoes, eh?*" For, had not the gipsies learned the art of deforming children's faces that they might be picturesque, comic or magnificent in manhood! Well, Rimbaud, for his part, would even implant warts upon his visage, to deform it. "*I say that you must be a Seer—make yourself a Seer!*"

The distortion of the physiognomy is but a sign of the alteration of the soul that was desired. (Anything to escape from the soul which the age and the environment molded!) The poet became a Seer, he continues, "by a long, immense and deliberate *disordering* of all his senses. He seeks all forms of love, of suffering, of madness. . . . He uses all poisons on himself, keeping only the quintessences of them. Ineffable torture, for which all his faith is

14

needed, all his superhuman strength, and in the course of which he comes to stand forth as the great invalid, the great criminal, the great accursed one— and the supreme savant!—for he arrives at the *unknown!*—since he has cultivated his soul, already richer than all others."

The formula of genius, as it came to Rimbaud so early in life, implied the fierce, single-minded development of the self at all costs; it implied, above all, the abandonment of known landmarks. Life was to be a perpetual inventing of new experiences, an eternal exploration, a supreme trial of the soul. Such an anarchic doctrine invites the strong soul to run extreme dangers; but it may become sinister or deadly in the hands of the weak whose worldly experiments are not dictated by intellectual boldness. For these, the preoccupation with self and with the senses does literally become a stunting deformation; it becomes simply a game of "madder music and madder wine," an obsession with death, rather than life. We think of poor Verlaine, whom Rimbaud sardonically promised to restore to his "original state as a child of the sun"; we think of the various lyricists of the *fin du siecle*, French and English, who expired in the gutter; we think of various suicides—even the lurid end of a recent American poet—and are made aware of the danger of Rimbaud's message. Rimbaud, in 1871, in an era of disastrous war and frustrated revolution, was aware of the absolute necessity of divorcing himself from contemporary values, like so many others. His convictions were negative, one might say: the more absolute his escape from the world about him, the more firmly insured were his visions. He tried, as if by a great wager, to bring about some "monstrous" change in himself, so that he might once more extend human expression and human values. (One remembers that he was for a moment one of the *communards* of '71; he was an infidel of the Church, a rebel against his mother and society.) But he was quite alone with his visions, like Blake; he had no common currency of speech that might bring him the companionship of his fellows.

"The poet comes to the *unknown*," his letter continues; "and when maddened, he ends by losing all understanding of his visions, still he has seen them, hasn't he? Let him burst with his palpitations—with the unheard of, nameless things he has seen. Then let other horrible workers come after him; they will begin at the horizons where he expired!"

* * *

It is as if in his absolute revolt, the poet turns to Nature, "pure and free," augments, sharpens, all his senses, seeking at one stroke to penetrate universal mysteries. That Rimbaud had taken the path of the mystic we perceive from the closing lines of his letter which refer to the "language" of the future poet. "*All language being idea*," he ends, "the day of the universal language will come."

Baudelaire too had taken this path of the mystic of poetry; Baudelaire, whom Rimbaud termed,

I

THE ADVENTURE IN IDEAS

☆ **I** ☆

THE INFANT PRODIGY

JEAN-ARTHUR RIMBAUD was born in Charleville, in the Ardennes, October 20th, 1854. Charleville and Mézières are twin cities whose every alley he explored and where he passed his impatient boyhood. Mézières, fortress and seat of the prefecture, its ancient citadel enclosed within ramparts once defended by the Chevalier Bayard, had become the home of bureaucrats and petty officials, and slept peacefully in the shadow of her tall cathedral. Charleville, her young rival, was already richer and more populous, proud of her commerce and industry, flourishing under the rule of her garrulous and enterprising middle classes. Neither city can claim Rimbaud as her own. He did not love them.

Both towns are situated on the banks of a lovely river, whose silver meanderings his eye would follow longingly—eternal invitation to wander! The Meuse, coming from the east at this point, just touches Mézières and then swerves aside; it winds around the peninsula of Saint-Julien, digresses whimsically, and then returns a second time to caress its moldy

27

ramparts. From there it flows on toward Charleville, gains the passes of the Ardennes, and flows toward the north amid the blue rocks, the grottoes and the woods of its romantic valley. Insensitive in general to the misty harmonies of his native soil, Rimbaud retained only one memory: the song of the river, the call of the waters in flight toward the unknown.

With every fiber in his body he would respond to this imperious call. Like Verlaine, he was an army officer's son; and the spirit of his father, a Burgundian of Provençal extraction, clashed sharply with the rigid self-restraint of the old Ardennes folk. The father was an adventurer, with all the daring and vivacity of the country of wine and sunlight. Awarded a commission by the Duc d'Aumale after serving in the ranks, Captain Rimbaud had campaigned in Algeria with the Chasseurs d'Orléans, and had led, before his marriage, the free and boisterous camp life of a soldier in Northern Africa. On his return to France, he found that he got on very poorly with his wife, whose severity sorely tried his impulsive and restless nature. Immediately after the birth of his second son, Arthur, he left France to take part in the Crimean War. Returning again, he dragged his growing family moodily from garrison to garrison, until he quit them finally for the Italian campaign. In 1860 his wife obtained a permanent separation, and came back to Charleville, where her fifth child, Isabelle, the poet's favorite sister, was born.

The poet was destined to have more than one fea-

Cachant de maigres doigts jaunes et noires de boue
Sous des habits puant la foire, et tout vieillots.

Hiding their skinny fingers, yellow-black with mud,
Beneath clothes that stank of the market, and all
tattered.

The home atmosphere at this time was very de-
pressing. Rimbaud was continually deceiving his
mother in order to play with companions who were
never considered "nice enough." It was a rule that
the neighbors' children were never to enter the
apartment. Mme. Rimbaud was very careful. Her
two sons and her two daughters (the third daughter
died at an early age) were supposed to play to-
gether "nicely" . . . and without toys! What a
sorry quartet they made! But the boy scoffed at
his mother's interdictions.

Quand venait, l'oeil brun, folle, en robes d'indiennes
—Huit ans—la fille des ouvriers d'à côté,
La petite brutale, et qu'elle avait sauté,
Dans un coin, sur son dos, en secouant ses tresses,
Et qu'il était sous elle, il lui mordait les fesses,
Car elle ne portait jamais de pantalons,
Et par elle meurtri des poings et des talons,
Remportait les saveurs de sa peau dans sa chambre.

When the little girl of laborers near-by
—Eight years—came, all wild, clad in India cloth,
The little beast, and when in a corner she had leaped
Upon his back, tossing her locks, he found
Himself beneath her, and bit her little shanks,
For never did she wear pantaloons!
And then, gashed by her heels and by her fists,
He would bring back to his room the savor of her skin.

33

Every Sunday, as my old friend Louis Pierquin has told me, Mme. Rimbaud used to attend eleven o'clock mass in the new parish church. She appeared there majestically, with her children: the two little girls in front, Vitalie and Isabelle, holding each other by the hand; the two boys in back, Frédéric and Arthur, each one carrying a blue cotton umbrella. Soberly and decently clad, carrying herself with dignity, the mother brought up the rear. The little ones were neatly dressed, with round hats and starched white Buster Brown collars, heavy shoes, and clothes of an old-fashioned cut.

The same ceremonial order was observed when the family went to market. They were an object of curiosity to the passers-by and to the shop-keepers. On market days the Place Ducale contained within the cold and noble disposition of its twenty-four Louis Treize pavilions, a whole swarming and busy population, and this unique procession threaded its impeccable way among the tents, the piled-up merchandise, the carts of second-hand goods and early spring vegetables, under a fire of ironical comments.

Sunday was a terrible day, a day from which play and noise were strictly banished. No distractions were allowed. No relaxation. Somber grayness unrelieved, from which he could escape only in imagination.

> *Il rêvait la prairie amoureuse, où les houles*
> *Lumineuses, parfums sains, pubescences d'or,*
> *Font leur remuement calme et prennent leur essor!*

He dreamt about the loving prairie, where luminous
Billows, wholesome scents, golden down
Carry on their calm stirrings and take their flight.

Then he throws himself upon his book of adventure, with its fascinating colored engravings.

Il lisait son roman sans cesse médité,
Pleins de lourds ciels ocreux et de forets noyées
De fleurs de chair au bois sidéral déployées.

He read his novel unremittingly,
Full of thick ocreous clouds and submerged forests,
Of fleshy flowers unfolded in the starry wood.

And, in the bare blue room with its high ceilings, "bitterly damp," behind the eternally closed shutters, his dream world prevailed, and wove its spell of enchantment about him.

However, in 1862 the family moved once again, for Mme. Rimbaud could not get on with any of her neighbors. They migrated to a somewhat more respectable neighborhood in the Cour d'Orléans, "under-the-trees," as it is still commonly called in Charleville. It was a pleasant walk, broad and airy, lined with small private houses, and bordered with chestnut trees. At that same time the boys entered the Rossat school, a free secular academy where they began their Latin. Rimbaud was then eight years old.

In one of his notebooks of the year 1862, a curious narrative has been found, in which we see a feeling for nature that is astonishingly precocious

35

despite a certain awkward vivacity, mingled with an instinctive revolt against examinations and books:

"The refreshing wind agitated the leaves of the trees with a rustling almost like that of the silvery waters of the brook at my feet. The ferns bowed their green heads before the wind. I fell asleep, but not before slaking my thirst at the running brook." The tale, incoherent as it is, ends with a comical childish invective against the study of Greek, Latin, history and geography. Here we have already "the importunate child," swearing and blaspheming, whose sarcasms were later to annoy the bourgeois . . . and the Parnassians. "Ah, *saperlipote de saperlipopette! Sapristi!* I shall live on my income; there's no use wearing out one's trousers on school benches, *saperlipopettouille!*"

Eight years old! One marvels.

However, wearing out his trousers on classroom benches is just what he is to do, like a very good boy. He is proud, and that explains his youthful industry, his scholastic triumphs. At ten, he entered the seventh form of the Charleville Collège.

At that time the college was situated at the Place du Saint-Sépulcre near the Meuse, a deserted and silent esplanade that bordered a convent of the same name, a seminary, and several tanneries. At the river's bank a boat was moored. Here the boy loved to sit by himself, while waiting for the bell to admit the day scholars. Ernest Delahaye, who was his best friend and most faithful biographer, remembers having seen him there one day, "examining with a long, delighted glance the agitated rippling of the water, the torn grasses, the floating débris, the submerged weeds only half-visible, all the changing, indecisive, mysterious forms and colors." It was here that the poet was awakened, the poet who was to write the *Bateau Ivre*.

But his love of solitude and revery, his more introspective tendency did not affect his application to his studies. On the contrary, he worked so rapidly and so well that he finished his seventh form in less than three months. In his Sixth form, he amazed his teachers by writing, spontaneously—Ah, *saperlipopette!*—a summary of all ancient history.

There is something compensatory, after all, in being the brightest student in one's school. To be at the "head of the class" helps one forget humiliations at home, permits at least in school the exercise of that will which must so often bend beneath the maternal will.

"Rimbaud," writes Delahaye, "whose name was destined to appear so frequently in the prize-lists of Charleville Collège, took his first prizes in catechism, and the chaplain was the first of his instructors to mention him with just pride. His brilliance in religious instruction was not due either to docility or to keenness of memory. At the age of twelve, faith burned in him; his piety was so exalted that he longed for martyrdom.

"One Sunday, as the pupils were leaving chapel, the usher being absent by some chance or perhaps too far away to see what was going on near the door, the 'big boys' hastened to exhibit their vivid sense of humor (so habitual when the beard first begins to prick the chin) by dabbling with delight in the font, and throwing holy water in each other's faces . . . and other joyous impieties. Rimbaud, small as he was, reared in fury at the sight of the sacrilege; he threw himself on them, tried to push them away, took their blows, answered with clenched fists as best he could, took more, persisted, scratching and biting until the intervention of authority put everybody under discipline. This battle earned for him the soubriquet of 'dirty little bigot,' which he accepted with pride."

His faith did not last. He himself admitted that he was locked up "in the garret" at the end of that year, for having been discovered by his mother reading an impious book. The yeast of liberty began rising in him:

> *Et la mère fermant le livre du devoir*
> *S'en allait, satisfaite et tres fière, sans voir*
> *Dans ses yeux bleus et sous le front plein d'éminences*
> *L'âme de son enfant livrée aux répugnances.*

> And his mother, closing the book of duty
> Went off, contented and quite proud, never seeing
> In his blue eyes and in his brow's eminence
> The soul of her child delivered to repugnance.

Without seeing? It was not long before she began to open her eyes. Her son's will clashed with her own at every turn. They defied each other, they fought constantly. The struggle went on every day, sometimes muffled, sometimes open. One day Rimbaud expressed a desire to study music, the piano. She refused flatly. "It's only a caprice, a whim on your part! We have enough expenses!" The lad refused to admit that he was beaten. During his mother's absence one day, alone, and clinging to his idea, he cut up the dining-room table in the shape of a piano. On his mother's return, what a storm, what scoldings! Rimbaud would not give in. "If you don't rent a piano for me, you had better look after your other furniture." Finally she had to capitulate, for she was a careful housekeeper.

Fortunately, the school relieved her of her son the greater part of the day. Besides, the child was brilliantly successful at his studies. While his elder brother, Frédéric, was left back in the sixth Form, Arthur skipped the fifth, and was ranked, almost immediately, among the best students of the fourth. He acquainted himself rapidly with Latin prosody, and became passionately interested in Virgil.

His instructor was a severe old man, M. Pérette, nicknamed "Father Bos," because of the vigor with which he used to scan the accusative plural, while hammering out the rhythm with his fist on the arm-chair: "*Flammarumque globos . . . debellare superbos,* etc." Scolding and pedantic, he was the butt of Rimbaud's waggish tricks. As the teacher was hard of hearing, the boy amused himself by punning over his recitations and mutilating his Latin. The end of Virgil's verse: "*debellare superbos,*" was transformed, to the great amusement of the class, into *"degueulare superbos."* But despite his tricks, Rimbaud had won the affection of the principal, M. Desdruets. However, even that respectable administrator, who looked so much like Mirabeau and had the grand manner of the Old Régime, was sometimes given to doubts about him. "Nothing of the usual sort," he used to say, "will take root in that brain. He will have either a genius for good or a genius for evil." But secretly he hoped that under his tutelage the child would develop into a good genius, and so he encouraged and stimulated him in his work.

On the other hand, M. Pérette did not share either the illusions or the kindness of the principal. "I don't like his eyes and his smile," he would grumble, shaking his head with its white whiskers, and looking over the rims of his spectacles. "As smart as you like, but he'll come to no good end."

At that time the Charleville Collège used to admit within the enclosure of its red brick fences, behind its moldy and polished walls, the pupils of the little seminary next door. They would come, dressed in their cassocks, to take certain courses. Between them and the collegians there was bitter rivalry, and Rimbaud used to take pride in eliminating these formidable competitors, among whom was—curiously enough—the future popular novelist Jules Mary. And of course they all detested Rimbaud cordially.

His former instructor, Georges Izambard, of

whom I shall soon speak again, tells the following anecdote. "One day, when the class was assembled in the amphitheater, during the dull calm of Latin composition, a sharp voice arose from one of the higher tiers: 'Monsieur, Rimbaud is cheating! He just passed a paper to his neighbor.' I leaped forward, grabbed the evidence and held it out to prove to the class that there was nothing suspicious in it. But Rimbaud had already half lifted himself from his seat, and with a grand, sweeping gesture had thrown his Thesaurus at the babbler's head. . . . 'Oh,' I said, in a tone of suppressed anger, which relieved me from having to take sterner measures (for, had I been a student, I should have done the same thing). My Rimbaud sat down again, stoical and disdainful, with the air of one who sings under torture. The incident had no further consequences."

After all, who could not forgive him? He astonished both his instructors and his fellow-students by his prodigious gifts. To be sure, he rebelled against mathematics, or rather, he despised it—and yet how passionately he was to devote himself to it twenty years later. But what brilliant feats in literature! During the science classes, in which he was not very much interested, he used to do the required exercises in Latin verse for his friends. "While one of us would be demonstrating some geometry theorem at the blackboard," wrote one of his class-mates, "Rimbaud would patch together in a moment a number of Latin verses. Each boy got his own. The subject was the same, but the composition, the ideas, the development were so varied that the instructor could not see the hand of the same workman in each. It was a wonderful *tour de force*."

It has often been told how impudently and with what amazing ease he carried off the first prize in Latin verse at the Academic Competition of 1869 (held by the University of Lille among the schools of Northern France.) The subject, Jugurtha, had dismayed the contestants. "What a subject, indeed! We weren't prepared for anything of the sort! First of all we were expected to know something about Jugurtha. We had anticipated a subject of current interest, the Universal Exposition for example, etc., etc." Tongues wagged, but no pen began to move. One can imagine the boys shut in behind their polished oaken desks, notched by successive generations of scholars, wiping their pens on their black sateen sleeves, yawning, stretching, biting their nails, whispering to each other in their surprise and their helplessness.

Rimbaud does not stir. He is silent as usual. His elbows spread out, his chin in his hand, his eyes fixed, his expression sour (as shown later in the canvas of Fantin-Latour) he writes nothing, seems asleep. The principal arrives. The good fellow is pained to see the blank paper at Rimbaud's desk. "What? You too? Then you are no smarter than the rest?" The boy grumbles his answer, "I'm hungry." Perfectly possible, since the contest had opened at six o'clock in the morning, and it is now nine. Let him have something to eat! One must be careful about this young colt, this thoroughbred born for the race-track. Enter then the janitor, Father Chocal, dragging his feet, his cap greasy and limp, wearing his stiff blue smock, and carrying a covered basket from which he extracts enormous slices of bread and butter. The other boys burst into laughter. Rimbaud eats contemptuously, a mischievous glint in his eye, and, having swallowed the last bite, throws himself on his paper and writes his Latin verses at one stroke:

Nascitur Arabis ingens in collibus infans. . . .

Everything, memories of his reading, of the Algerian campaign, comparisons with Abd-el-kadir, fancies of "the poet of seven years," all this is crowded in, arranged, made definite. To the devil with the *Gradus.* As if he needed that cumbersome old book! Long before the end of the competition he goes up to the desk and places his manuscript before the examiner. Eighty Latin verses, "forceful and sonorous!" More than enough to save the honor of the college. The principal is delighted. But M. Pérette, when told of Rimbaud's achievement, continues to shake his head . . . "As smart as you like, but he'll come to no good end!"

During the same year—he was then fifteen years old—Rimbaud wrote his first (known) verses in French, the *Etrennes des Orphelins.*

La chambre est pleine d'ombre. On entend vaguement
De deux enfants le triste et doux chuchotement,
Leur front se penche, encore alourdi par le rêve,
Sous le long rideau blanc qui tremble et se soulève.
Au dehors, les oiseaux se rapprochent frileux
Leur aile s'engourdit sous le ton gris des cieux.
Et la nouvelle année, à la suite brumeuse,
Laissant tomber les plis de sa robe neigeuse,
Sourit avec des pleurs et chante en grelottant. . . .

The room is full of shadow. Vaguely is heard
The soft and sad whisperings of two children,
Their heads, bent forward, nod, still heavy with dream,
Under the long white curtain that flaps and trembles.
Without the chilly birds approach each other
Their wings as if benumbed under the grey-toned skies.
And the New Year, after fog and mist,
Drops the folds of her snowy robes,
Smiles through her tears and sings as she shudders. . . .

O New Year's bells in the frosty Ardennes, O bitter dawn rising on the extinguished hearth, dreams of motherless children, little wooden shoes empty beside the fireplace, Christmas without a Christmas tree, Epiphany without the Magi, awakening without gifts! As far as one can judge from this simple, childlike, and somewhat awkward poem, Rimbaud was not yet, at the age of fifteen or sixteen, the adventurous and brutal boy described by Verlaine in *les Hommes d'Aujourd'hui.* To be sure, at about this time he was beginning to take long walks along the "Meuse, which, flowing so gently through the city, becomes a raging torrent as it escapes into the country—past the Culbute with its trim vistas, and the pretty woods of les Havetières." Above all he would make excursions to the Belgian border, where, inveterate smoker that he was, he went to look for contraband tobacco in the very teeth of the revenue officers.

But if his brutality and venturesomeness at this stage were not specially marked, neither was he the perfect child, the pride of his mother, as Paterne Berrichon portrays him. He was a greedy adolescent, busy and headstrong, with a difficult character, but very studious; at once the honor and the torment of Charleville Collège. However, although his mind had bloomed splendidly, his true nature was still dormant. Two things were needed to awaken it; the influence of a perspicacious teacher, and the outbreak of the war.

II

THE REBEL

T HE year 1869 brought a new spirit to the school
in the person of Georges Izambard, a young
instructor in Rhetoric. Paterne Berrichon has re-
proached him, very unjustly, for having incited
Rimbaud to revolt. Inspired by romantic and re-
publican ideas, which he may or may not have ex-
pounded in class, he is supposed by Berrichon to
have poured his Jacobin and equalitarian theories
into the receptive ear of young Rimbaud. To this
accusation the teacher has given a formal denial:
"I never once spoke of politics to Rimbaud. I was
his friend, but also his teacher. I willingly gave him
lessons—without pay—whenever he asked for them.
I made him feel free to call upon me as much as he
wished by explaining that I was rewarded for it all
by his remarkable academic triumphs. When school
was over he would often wait for me at the gate to
accompany me home. Along the way we had many
long conversations about poets and poetry, as that
was all that interested him."

Without casting any doubts on the sincerity of
M. Izambard, it is impossible to believe that his

liberal opinions did not have a strong influence out-
side of the class-room. He personified, in that last
year of the Empire, the courage and independence
of the young republican party. The assassination
of Victor Noir and the arrest of Rochefort had
repercussions throughout the whole school system.
La Lanterne was being read in secret by all the
students and when the liberal Rhetoric instructor
first crossed the threshold of Charleville Collège, he
seemed like a breath of fresh air in a musty house.

He was then twenty-one years old. Enthusiastic
and friendly, he soon discovered Rimbaud's excep-
tional intelligence. Underneath the demeanor of
the student who seemed "somewhat self-conscious,
though docile and gentle, with his clean finger-nails,
neat note-books, and his unusually correct exer-
cises," he could detect the "true intellectual, all
vibrant with ideal passions." The boy's voracious
mind appealed to him strongly, and Rimbaud re-
turned his affection with fervor. Chafing in the
confined air of his home, he attached himself to
Izambard, sought him out everywhere, borrowed
books of him.

Mme. Rimbaud began to take notice of this. De-
cidedly, she thought, this young instructor boded
no good for her. One day she found her son deep
in a volume by Victor Hugo (which she wrote
Hugo*t*). She tore it from his hands and reported her
discovery to the principal. Then she sat down and
wrote M. Izambard an oblique and somewhat hypo-
critical letter: "You know better than I that great

care ought to be exercised in selecting books for children. And so I prefer to believe that Arthur must have obtained this one without your knowledge."

The book in question was not *Les Misérables*, as she believed and as her son-in-law Paterne Berrichon afterward related. On the suggestion of the principal (who was quite sympathetic to the teacher), M. Izambard went to see Mme. Rimbaud to clear himself. The book had really been *Nôtre-Dame de Paris*, and he had lent it to his pupil for local color on the period of Villon. But the angry virago included all the works of Victor Hugo in a common execration. "An author who is on the Index? Imagine it! How can any one advise reading such things?" Both teacher and pupil were severely reprimanded.

Futile remonstrance, vain precautions! Rimbaud managed somehow to get hold of the books he wanted. What marvelous books! No more expurgated classics, prize-books in red-gold bindings, special editions for institutions of Christian learning, no more Annals of the Propagation of the Faith.

He was reading Juvenal and Lucretius, Rabelais and Villon, Baudelaire and Banville, Saint-Simon and Proudhon. He plunged into the history of the French Revolution, devoured Thiers' fat volumes, Lamartine, Michelet, lingering by preference over the account of the Revolution by Louis Blanc. And soon he strutted and swelled with the pride of his young impiety and anarchism. He turned up his

48

nose in class, cursed Napoleon who had "so stupidly made the Revolution fail of its purpose," inserted into his themes appeals for uprisings, invocations to Robespierre, to Saint-Just, to Couthon; and he embarrassed his history professor by asking insidious questions about St. Bartholomew's Eve or the *Dragonnades.* Finally, little by little, he began to cut certain courses which bored him.

On the other hand, his frequent long walks on the banks of the Meuse with M. Izambard were enlivened by interminable literary discussions. Rimbaud now heard the call of his true vocation. To be a poet—ah, yes—like Villon, whom he had portrayed with such vividness and challenge in his composition for the rhetoric class, called "Letter from Charles of Orleans to Louis XI."

"Is it not good, Sire, under the trees, when the skies are clad in blue, when the bright sun shines, to speak sweet rondels and sing lovely ballads high and clear?" He also, like the imprisoned poet, held out his arms toward life, toward all life, saying: "Hurrah for the ladies with their high-boned collars decked in all their finery and embroidery! But hurrah also for bawdy taverns, full of the cries of drinkers banging their pewter pots together and often their rapiers!" And, as if he already had a presentiment of his own destiny, he took up the defense of all dreamers and poets—they who with eyes uplifted to the stars, stumble in the ditch. "Poets, you see, are not of this world. Permit them to live strange lives, let them be cold and hungry,

49

let them run, love and sing. Mad children, they are as rich as Jacques Coeur, for their souls are full of songs, songs that laugh and weep, and that make us laugh and weep."

At this time, too, he was writing verses passionately. His mathematics instructor discovered him more than once in class absorbed in the composition of some poem. He even went so far as to do into French verse the required translations from Latin poetry. In turn under Romantic and Parnassian influence, he wrote during this year *Le Forgeron*, *Ophélie*, *Sensation*, *Soleil et chair*.

In *Le Forgeron* (written in April, 1870) in one epic page worthy of Hugo's *Chatiments*, he contrasts superbly the defeated Old Régime and the victorious Revolution, on that day when Louis XVI had to don the Phrygian cap:

> *Et dans la grande cour, dans les appartements*
> *Où Paris haletait avec des hurlements,*
> *Un frisson secoua l'immense populace.*
> *Alors de sa main large et superbe de crasse,*
> *Bien que le roi ventru suât, le forgeron,*
> *Terrible, lui jeta le bonnet rouge au front.*

> And in the vast courtyard, in those halls
> Where all Paris panted with its shouting,
> A shudder now swept o'er the immense populace.
> Then with his broad hand, superbly filthy,
> While the pot-bellied king sweated, the mighty smith
> Clapped the red bonnet upon his head.

Undoubtedly this is pure Victor Hugo. But it has something else besides. Rimbaud had seen that blacksmith. One evening he had stumbled over a drunken workman lying prostrate near a doorway in a Charleville street, repeating idiotically to himself: "I'm drunk, I'm drunk." This was the original impulse for the poem. His imagination, working over this, produced those magnificent and visionary stanzas which indicate a singularly rich and powerful inspiration: "This is drunkenness, Sire, it bubbles over the walls, it rises, it brims. . . ." The theme is developed with the aid of florid romantic metaphors, yet enhanced also by picturesque inventions of his own, and enlivened by the rude, fresh tones of a truly incendiary poetry.

Then there is *Ophélie*, an astonishingly brilliant translation of Latin verses on an assigned subject, which calls to mind the preciose painting of Millais. Like the canvases of the Pre-Raphaelite painter, this poem trembles everywhere with reflections and breezes, it is steeped in foliage and sunlight. But from this little pastoral there rises a song of praise to nature, a hymn of longing for freedom and infinite space.

O pale Ophélie, belle comme la neige,
Oui, tu mourus, enfant, par un fleuve emporté!
C'est que les vents tombant des grands monts de Norvège
T'avaient parlé tout bas de l'âpre liberté! . . .

O pale Ophelia, fair as the snow,
Yes, thou diest, child, borne off by a river!
The winds falling from the Norway peaks
Had whispered to thee once of bitter liberty! . . .

51

The same flight toward a dream world and toward the limitless, the same intoxication with nature is expressed in the poem *Sensation*, in which the child sings of his walks in the country around Charleville.

> *Par les soirs bleus d'été, j'irai dans les sentiers,*
> *Picoté par les blés, fouler l'herbe menue;*
> *Rêveur, j'en sentirai la fraîcheur à mes pieds,*
> *Je laisserai le vent baigner ma tête nue.*

> On blue summer nights I'll wander down the lanes,
> Pricked by the wheat, treading the fine grass;
> Dreaming, I shall feel the freshness at my feet
> Letting the winds bathe my bare head.

This love of nature already has its philosophical justification, and in the poem *Soleil et chair* we read a pantheistic profession of faith. Here the influence of Théodore de Banville's *l'Exil des dieux* can easily be detected. Rimbaud (he is not yet sixteen!) calls on man to emancipate himself from Christianity and return to nature. God is the great longing eternally recreating the world:

> Flesh, marble, flower, Venus, in thee I believe!

Aphrodite will end by conquering "the other god" and will arise, throwing upon the vast universe

> Infinite love in an infinite smile

And the world will answer, will vibrate "like an immense lyre in the shudder of an immense kiss."

At bottom everything is contained within this fermenting soul: Rimbaud is "bohemian," revolutionary, and pantheistic. But can anyone be a bohemian with impunity in Charleville? Deliberately he neglects his appearance, his manners—he grows nervous (the awkward age, probably?) At the period of puberty, his genius is distilled out of its youthful components; his style, formerly expressed in the vague and sad music of *Ophélie*, the song of the breezes, of the willows and reeds, gradually assumes a tone of great pride, a more biting, more aggressive accent. He develops a cloacal vocabulary now, filthy, brutal, abusive. In conversation he is grandly obscene, exhibiting a flair for the coarse and the scatological. He withdraws before no depths of cynicism, as can be seen from his poetry. Nothing is more striking, more characteristic than the poem written in July, 1870: *Le Chatiment de Tartuffe*, "yellow, drooling his faith from his toothless mouth"; and the repulsive Venus Anadyomene, half-risen from her rusty green bathtub, "showing somewhat ill-concealed deficiencies and with a hideous ulcer flowering at her anus!"

Where now are those white images of the shores of Hellas, or of the Norwegian sea, of tall Ariadne, and gentle Ophelia? Where are those sails of Theseus, those trembling willows, water-lilies, golden stars? Rimbaud has forgotten them! Savagely he tramples the gardens of Parnassus and of Romanticism, wrecking the neat flower-beds of the bourgeoisie. This "shabby student" has become a crying scandal. Notice how roughly he handles his fellow-citizens, the placid idlers who come of evenings to listen to the music at the Place de la Gare!

Sur la place taillée en mesquines pelouses
Square où tout est correct, les arbres et les fleurs
Tous les bourgeois poussifs qu'étranglent les chaleurs
Portent, les jeudis soirs, leurs bêtises jalouses.

To the little square, cut into prim lawns,
A park whose trees and flowers are all correct,
The pursy citizens come, strangled by the heat,
On Thursday nights, bearing their sordid envies. . . .

They are all there, the notary with his strange watch-charms, the bespectacled well-to-do, the bloated bureaucrats, "dragging their fat wives along," the "retired grocers who poke in the dirt with their club-headed canes," the burgher with bright-colored buttons over his "Flemish paunch," all those who regard the poet mistrustfully, and whom he defies with his mischievous glance. His own friends are elsewhere. . . .

July—August 1870! These are the last concerts of the military band! The war breaks out. Rimbaud's vibrant revolutionary passion overflows. However, this year is crowned with scholastic triumphs for him. On the 17th of July he wins first prize in Latin poetry at the Academic Competition, the subject so suited to his talents being: "Sancho Panza's apostrophe to his Ass." Prize-day at the College has great honors for him: first prize for general excellence, first prize in Latin composition, first prize in French composition, first prize in Greek translation, etc. At this time, writes Ernest Delahaye ironically, "we students had the bright idea of sacrificing our prizes and offering their value to the government. A grandiloquent letter was addressed to the minister and covered with signatures. But Rimbaud refused to add his to the rest." This is purely a political manifestation on his part, because at bottom he scoffs at such prizes. What do all these laurels mean to him! Nonsensical, childish trinkets! He champs at the bit still restraining him. War means deliverance, liberty for him, the greater future. He listens impatiently to the speech of the imperial prosecutor, who, while presiding over the prize-day exercises on the 6th of August, expresses the good wishes of the loyal Charleville population for their "august sovereign." M. Izambard is already on his vacation at Douai. Rimbaud remains alone, his soul in torment, in the midst of his awards and medals.

And now comes bad news. Crowds mass before the dispatches announcing the first French reverses at Froeschviller and Forbach, but their agitation arouses only sarcasm in the young man! "The blessed people!" he writes to M. Izambard, August 25th, "these bullies with pat phrases in their mouths, act otherwise than the besieged of Metz and Strasbourg. They are frightful, these retired grocers who don the uniform again! It is sickening, it simply stinks, the way those notaries, glaziers, collectors, carpenters, and all those fat bellies with their rifles across their chests go playing at super-patriotism around the gates of Mézières. My country rises up! . . . Personally, I would rather see her sitting down; don't shift your feet, that's my principle . . . I am adrift, sick, furious, stupid, upset. I have longed for sunbaths, protracted walks, rest, travel, adventures, bohemianism in fact. But above all I have longed for newspapers, books . . . Nothing, nothing! Our bookshops no longer receive any shipments; Paris doesn't care what happens to us —not a single new book! This is deadly.

"In the matter of newspapers, here I am reduced to reading the honorable *Courrier des Ardennes,* whose owner, managing editor, business manager, editor-in-chief and sole editor are A. Pouillard! This newspaper summarizes the aspirations, the desires and the opinions of the local population. Just think of it! It's a nice business! A man is exiled in his own country!!!"

Izambard had left the key of his room and of his private library with Rimbaud. But this resource is quickly exhausted. "I have read all your books, all of them. Three days ago I got to *les Epreuves,* then to *les Glaneuses*—yes, I reread that thing— and then there was nothing left . . . I caught sight of Don Quixote yesterday; I spent all of two hours looking over the woodcuts by Doré. Now I have nothing more."

Four days after the writing of this letter, the 29th of August, Mme. Rimbaud was taking a walk with her children in the meadows between Charleville and Mézières. (She had moved again, and her family was then installed not far away, on the Quai de la Madeleine, opposite the Meuse and Mont Olympe.) It was warm; there was a storm threatening. Paterne Berrichon has tried to reconstruct the scene from a symbolic interpretation of *Les Illuminations:* the little girls, in faded green dresses, "were reading their red-morocco bound book" under the willows, among the blossoming foliage. Erect, proud, "her parasol in her hand, treading the flowery sward," the mother watched over her children. Suddenly Arthur got up to leave. "Where are you going?" "Back home, to look for another book." She is not worried: their apartment is quite near. "Don't dawdle, hurry up . . ." Hours pass. No one, no one comes. What has happened to him? . . . He does not return.

By now Mme. Rimbaud's anxiety was unfeigned. Was he the victim of some accident or was he up to some deviltry? And in that case, what idea could have possessed him? She could think of nothing that might have prepared her for so strange an action. Had he concealed his game? To be sure, he had seemed quite altered for the last while. His year of Rhetoric had tired, unnerved him. But despite these slight signs, and because she had no suspicion whatever of his really profound mental agitation, his mother was at her wits' end. She could not for a moment admit that he might have wished to put an end to her rigid guardianship.

Three weeks later she wrote to M. Izambard,

"Who can possibly conceive of the foolishness of that child, he who is usually so good and so calm? How could such madness have occurred to him?" So good? How the blind mother had mistaken hypocritical submission for the desired virtue. Yes, certainly, he had had armfuls of prizes. But he had sold them, the next day, for twenty francs!

As night came on, the anxiety of Mme. Rimbaud became madness. The Prussians were advancing, were making their way through the Ardennes. Their appearance near Sedan had just been announced. The day after Arthur's flight, on August 30th, the French army suffered a defeat at Beaumont. The night before, the most pessimistic rumors were flying around Charleville. What dreadful hours these were for Mme. Rimbaud![1]

"Dragging her little girls with her," wrote Paterne Berrichon, "she spent most of the night running through the streets of Charleville and Mézières in a state of indescribable anguish, asking in public-houses for news of Arthur, questioning groups of excited young men who were about to enroll as volunteers, searching the waiting-room at the railroad station, examining the banks of the Meuse for signs of him."

In vain! Her son was already far away. On that tragic night, as two great armies prepared for battle, the jolting train was carrying him swiftly, as if in flight, toward Paris. This departure marked

[1] Frédéric, his elder brother, had marched off to join the troops; and Arthur too, she feared, might have been seized with the war fever.—*Tr.*

the end of his studious childhood, the beginning of his vagabondage. His soul in revolt, he was on his way, across the invaded land, and the paths of the war.

☆ III ☆

IN THE PATH OF THE WAR

ON his arrival at the Gare de l'Est, Rimbaud was promptly arrested. His chubby cherubic head, his provincial accent, his white collar, his neat suit, did not, however, give him a very dangerous appearance. But to begin with, he had no ticket and refused to state his name and address. Then he irritated the imperial police by absurd blustering and insolent contempt in speaking of the imperial government. Finally, they found on him a mysterious notebook covered with hieroglyphics and very fine writing. These were only his poems, but the policemen could make nothing of them, decided that the notebook was indecipherable and therefore suspect, and sent the seditious youngster to the Mazas prison.

Once behind bars, his bravado deserts him. Is he then much less bold than he has pretended? His eyelids begin to brim with salt tears. Reduced to this state, he asks for paper and ink and writes three letters, one to his mother, one to the imperial prosecutor, and one to his good teacher at Douai. His note to the latter is both supplicating and bullying. One senses more than regret and fear in it. It is an admission of defeat, the desperate, humble and commanding appeal of a child who has lost his bearings.

"Oh!"—he writes on the 5th of September—"I depend on you as I do on my mother; you have always been a brother to me. I now earnestly implore that aid which you have always offered me. I have written to my mother, to the imperial prosecutor, to the chief of police in Charleville. If you receive no word from me by Wednesday before the train leaves Douai for Paris, take that train, come here to claim me by letter or by appearing yourself before the prosecutor, by answering for me, by paying my debt! Do everything in your power, and when you receive this letter, write, yourself, I command you, write to my poor mother (Quai de la Madeleine, 5, Charleville) to console her! Write me also. Do everything! I love you now like a brother; I shall love you like a father."

At the same time, the prison warden also wrote to M. Izambard to beg him to take over the fugitive. The teacher agreed, sent the cost of the trip to Paris, and a few days later received his sheepish pupil at his own home, "defeated, but happy all the same to have gotten off so easily."

M. Izambard still has in his possession curious details, unpublished documents on this first sojourn at Douai, from about the 10th to the 25th of September, showing Rimbaud as a journalist and a member of the national guard. It was at this time that Rimbaud made the acquaintance of Paul Demeny, a young poet to whom he later sent letters which are of the utmost importance to us in our study of Rimbaud.

But how was he to be led back to the familial fold? As soon as Mme. Rimbaud was informed of his whereabouts, she wrote her son a letter of denunciation, brutal and unreasonably insulting to the man who had taken him in, "instead of throwing him out," as he deserved. Rimbaud became enraged, cursed, swore, doubled up his fists and declared that he would never return to Charleville. What was to be done? The teacher sacrificed his own feelings, forgot the mother's insinuations, and himself conducted the prodigal son back to the hearth.

"How pleasantly he was received, though, in the bosom of his family, the prodigal son! And I! I, who, innocent as a babe, had made the trip expressly to facilitate their demonstrations of joy. . . . You must have read, in Courteline, the scene of the gentleman who has found a watch which he takes to the police station, his heart in his mouth. It seems to him highly probable that he will be sent to the lock-up either as a thief or as a receiver of stolen goods. Very sharp, as usual, Mama Rimbaud administered a huge tongue-lashing to her little prodigy of a son and reprimanded me for my part in the matter in such terms that at first I just stood there, my mouth open, and then fled from the storm."

Any one could have foretold that Rimbaud would not long remain at home, under these conditions. Re-

turned the 27th of September, he fled again the 7th
of October, this time in the direction of Belgium.
Neither the Revolution nor literature called him
now. But he did have a plan in mind. He had had,
as classmate in school, young des Essarts, son of the
managing editor of one of the Charleroi newspapers.
Innocently he hoped to be engaged as an editor on
this journal. Probably this was only a roundabout
way of approaching literature, but anything was bet-
ter than moldering in Charleville!

Off he goes again then, this time on foot, along the
Meuse, whose wooded escarpments shine with au-
tumn gilding. Nouzon, Monthermé, the Mountain of
the Four Aymon brothers, the Mermaid Rocks of
the Meuse!—O living past of the Ardennes, murmur-
ing in the violet mist of your ravines, how far
this bitter traveler's thoughts were from you! What
cared he for the fair Yseult and her fatal lover?
What mattered to him the golden-antlered stag
caught in the crackling branches before Saint Hu-
bert? It was here that the charger, Bayard, carry-
ing the rebel brothers, crossed the river in one great
leap, in the very face of the Emperor Charles. There
is Revin, covered with slate-blue dust, spread out
within its watery ring, and there is the steep pile
of the "Malgré Tout" described by the good woman
of Nohant (George Sand). And was it not there that
the Crusaders on their return from the Holy Land
found their unfaithful spouses petrified on the banks
of the river? O legends, O memories, neither you nor

63

anything can hold this vagabond! Gripped by his fixed resolve, he plunges through the wild valley.

At Fumay he is entertained by another schoolmate, who gives him a bar of chocolate on his departure and a letter of introduction to a sergeant in the garrison at Givet, which is along Rimbaud's route. After a short stay in Vireux, he arrives at the old frontier town, his back broken with fatigue, his feet blistered, and proceeds immediately to the "*grand quartier,*" the huge white barracks stretched out along the Meuse, at the foot of the fort of Charlemont. As he cannot find the sergeant—who is absent on duty in the city—he lies down on the man's bed and manages to decamp the next morning before reveille without being seen. He crosses the boundary and takes the road to Charleroi. Painful stages these were, often made without a single halt for rest, his stomach empty or nearly so.

> *Depuis huit jours, j'avais déchiré mes bottines*
> *Aux cailloux des chemins; j'entrais à Charleroi*
> *Au cabaret vert, je demandais des tartines*
> *De beurre et du jambon. . . .*

> For a whole week I had been wearing out my boots
> On all the stony roads; I came to Charleroi,
> Entered the green tavern, and called for bread
> And ham and butter. . . .

The inscription at the head of the poem would indicate that he arrived in Charleroi at "five o'clock in the evening." The following morning he went to see M. des Essarts, editor and publisher of the *Journal de la Sambre*. He was a somewhat pompous man, kind and hospitable nevertheless. He invited Rimbaud to dine with his family. When they reached the dessert, Rimbaud began to hold forth on the supporters of the Empire in very offensive terms. The frightened host consequently withheld his answer to Rimbaud's request for a job until the next day. One can imagine what that answer was. "But my dear young man," he said, with that accent in his speech that Rimbaud found so funny, "you cannot really expect it. A self-respecting newspaper that has traditions to live up to . . . etc." The would-be journalist was firmly dismissed.

And now, how was he to live? His meager resources were exhausted. "That evening," he wrote, "I dined on the perfumes of roasting meat and fowl from the good kitchens of Charleroi, and a tablet of filthy chocolate that I ate in the moonlight." He was face to face with misery and hunger. Why should he tarry here any longer?

He starts out on the road to Brussels, spending his nights in the fields, under haystacks, sharing the soup of farmhands. It was at this time that he wrote *Buffet, Maline, Douaniers, Bohème.*

On his arrival in Brussels, tattered and emaciated, he sets about finding a friend of M. Izambard of whom he has heard by chance. The friend takes pity on him, lodges him for two days, buys him some new clothes and gives him a little money. Thanks to this slight subsidy, the vagabond takes the train and appears, for the second time, at Douai. His teacher is

65

away, but with his habitual lack of ceremony Rimbaud installs himself to await the return of Izambard.

"Rimbaud appeared before me," writes Izambard of this visit, "in a fashionable bat-wing collar, his chest covered with a reddish-brown silk cravat blinding in its effect, looking the perfect dandy." But the situation now is even more embarrassing than it was in September. M. Izambard does not wish to throw him out, and on the other hand he cannot keep him any longer without seeming to make himself an accomplice to the boy's escapades. He must therefore write again to Rimbaud's mother and ask her what she wishes him to do. While awaiting the answer, Rimbaud copies over his latest poems, impassively, on large sheets of foolscap, and only on one side, for "printer's copy must never be written on both sides." His mother's letter comes and tears him from his literary dreams. It contains "an express command to charge the police with bringing him home, at no expense to her. Special injunction against using other means." And so our proud fellow, his little bundle under his arm, is handed over to the police, carrying with him the last admonitions of the friend he was destined never to see again.

A few days later, November 2, he writes to Izambard, "I arrived at Charleville the day after I left you. My mother took me back, and here I am, altogether idle. My mother will not put me into school until January. Oh, well, I have kept my promise. I am dying, I am decaying in the midst of banality, viciousness, boredom. What do you expect? I have taken an awful liking to free liberty and a load of things that 'are really too silly,' aren't they? (Here he parodies his mother.) I should have gone off again today; I could have; I was newly clothed, I could have sold my watch and hurrah for liberty! Yet I stayed! I stayed! And I shall want to go again, many, many times. Come, grab your hat and coat, put your hands in your pockets and let's be off. But I'll stay, I'll stay! I know I didn't promise it. But I shall stay just to merit your affection. That is what you said. I shall merit it.

"The gratitude I feel toward you I shall not be able to express any more easily now than I could the other day; I shall prove it by my deeds. If there were something I could do for you I should be willing to die to do it. I give you my word." And he signs himself: "That heartless wretch, Rimbaud!"

Meanwhile the Germans are approaching Mézières. The officer in command of the town orders everything razed that might interfere with the defense. The people lay waste the public gardens and cut down the great lime-trees of the Bois d'Amour, near the village of Saint Julien. This is the period of the long walks Rimbaud describes in *Illuminations*.

He bids adieu to the fat and wrinkled gypsy hag of Belgium, the evenings passed in farm kitchens, "smelling of polishing wax and of fruits," legs stretched under the table with its colored dishes; gone are the heavy jokes exchanged with hostlers while emptying schooners of foamy beer, gone the oglings and the jostlings, the smutty hints that light up the eye of the servant, the "girl with the enormous breasts," who's not afraid of a little kiss. The poet now frequents a desolate country-side. "A swarm of yellow leaves surrounds the general's house. . . . You take the red path to arrive at the empty inn. The castle is for sale, the shutters have been taken down. The curé has carried off the keys of the church. Around the park the keepers' huts are uninhabited. . . ."

Ernest Delahaye has reported long conversations that he had with Rimbaud at this time among the pillaged gardens. "There is," he used to say, "some destruction that is necessary. There are old trees that must be cut down; there are time-honored abominations of which we shall lose the amiable usage. Over this very society in which we live men will use axes, hatchets, steam-rollers. Fortunes will be leveled and individual splendor laid low. Nothing will remain but nature."

And when his friend protested: "Where," he answered, "could you buy an object of luxury and art of a more delicate structure than an autumn flower?"

He was indifferent to the war and the rigors of winter. He went out walking every day on the earthworks so soon covered with snow, annoying the conscripts there on sentinel duty, and reciting poetry: "Hosannah to the lutes and the censers!" Or, in some cabin spared by the defense, snug in the depths of a garden near the frosted grillwork of the Bois d'Amour, immobile and as if insensible, he would crouch for long hours, smoking his pipe and reading Flaubert, Dickens, Banville or Leconte de Lisle.

Between times, tormented always by the demonic impulse to write, he sent his poems to the *Progrès des Ardennes*, a new democratic newspaper started by a photographer named Jacoby. He also, without any more success withal, submitted "pieces of prose" in which he insulted the man of Sedan (Napoleon III), and that old brute Bismarck, whom he represented as drunk, leaning over the map of France, coveting Paris. His scorn included those who invaded his country and those who did not know how to defend it.

It is at this time (November, 1870), that he wrote *Rages de César, l'Eclatante victoire de Sarrebrück* (after a Belgian engraving purchased in Charleroi) the pathetic *Dormeur du Val*, and that dreadful sonnet called *le Mal*.

> *Tandis que les crachats rouges de la mitraille*
> *Sifflent tout le jour par l'infini du ciel bleu,*
> *Qu'écarlates ou verts, près du roi qui les raille,*
> *Croulent les bataillons en masse dans le feu. . . .*
>
> *Il est un Dieu qui rit aux nappes damassées*
> *Des autels, a l'encens, aux grands calices d'or,*
> *Qui, dans le bercements des hosannas, s'endort.*
>
> *Et se réveille, quand des mères, ramassées*
> *Dans l'angoisse et pleurant sous leur vieux bonnets*
> *Lui donnent un gros sou lié dans leur mouchoir.*

69

And while the mitrailleuses spit red all day
Against the infinite blue of sky, before the ranting
    king,
The massed battalions, scarlet or green,
Crumple up under fire. . . .

There is a God who laughs over the damask cloth,
Over altars and incense and great golden chalices,
One who, cradled by Hosannas, falls asleep.

And then awakes to the wailing of mothers,
Assembled in their anguish and weeping under their
    worn bonnets,
Who bring him each a big penny folded in their hand-
    kerchiefs.

Fortunately there still remain a few rays of light in his darkened universe. His evil genius quits him occasionally, allowing him a few hours of respite. This "heartless wretch Rimbaud" no longer loves God, but he still loves some things. His nihilism is not universal: he still loves the poor, the humble, the unhappy, the rebels. He feels himself the brother of those "blackened men in smocks whom he sees in the tawny evening light, returning to their homes in the outskirts of the town." He still stops in the street to caress children crouched over a cellar-grill, "watching the baker making his heavy yellow bread!"

What a charming sight! With a friendly tap he greets poor urchins, children of working people, bent over the fragrant oven. With a masterly stroke of the pen, which reminded Verlaine of Goya's sketches, and with that warm, gentle coloring of the Dutch painters, he draws a picture of *les Effarés*, the little beggars of Charleville, the ones he used to know in the grimy rue Bourbon and who were so friendly to the "seven-year-old poet."

There is, as Verlaine has said, something indescribably tender, something of the air of a charming caricature, something warm and *good* in this poem. It gushes from a "pure, sounding spring." The rebellious spirit seems calm for a moment and sings. But the respite is only momentary. Again the horizon clouds over rapidly.

On the 20th of December Mézières was invested. The bombardment began on the 31st. Six thousand shells fell into the city and only one hundred and fifty cannon shots were returned. Of five hundred houses, three hundred and fifty were destroyed. In spite of the danger, Rimbaud wanted to go out that day, but his mother had locked the door and he could not escape before seven o'clock in the evening. The spectacle that Jules Mary found "horrible and magnificent" only disgusted Rimbaud. "It is ugly, ugly, without grandeur. *Une tortue dans du pétrol.*"

Then came the occupation with its succession of requisitions, petty annoyances, chores, its patrols and its parades. Sardonically he called Delahaye's attention to the method and discipline of the Germans, and when his friend sighed: "Ah, those people are by far our superiors!" he was revolted, and

71

prophetically uncovered their weakness: "But no, they are our inferiors. . . . The idiots! Behind their blaring trumpets and beating drums they will return to their own country to eat their sausages, believing that it is all over. But wait a little. Now they are all militarized from top to toe, and for a long time they will swallow all the rubbish of glory under treacherous masters who will never let go of them. . . . I can see from now the rule of iron and madness that will imprison all of German society. And all that merely to be crushed in the end by some coalition!" It was this same feeling that led him to defy a Prussian officer who was boasting of his prowess in battle at a café in the Petit-Bois quarter. "He listened, watching the man with his blue eyes in which a spark of fierce mockery was kindled, and soon became convulsed, slapping his knee and bursting into hysterical laughter."

The home of Ernest Delahaye at Mézières was burned in the bombardment, and he had to go to stay with relatives in a neighboring village. Rimbaud, who was not afraid to take long walks across the snow and the mud, used to go to see him in all weather. Then they would both go out together, roving the countryside in spite of the orders of the Germans to the contrary, splashing through the boggy roads and defying the patrols. "What did the defeat mean to us? Purification, overhauling, a new life. On this point we were carried away by enthusiasm. The sharp winter wind blowing flocks of dead leaves, powdered with frost, across the desolate fields, intoxicated us and carried our mad thoughts to the devil."

Their conversations were continued on certain days at Mézières, in the midst of the ruins. As the building of the War Council had been spared from the fire, Rimbaud installed himself with his friend on its gray stone steps one fine morning, and regaled him with a literary feast. The delicacy he offered was . . . *Les Châtiments* of Victor Hugo, published secretly in Belgium. They turned over the leaves of the little blue brochure with delight, and amused themselves by filling out the proper names which Hugo had indicated only by initials.

He also spent long hours at the municipal library of Charleville. He would bury himself there for whole days at a time, devouring the strangest works. Away with the classicists and romanticists, Corneille and Lamartine! Down with the Parnassians! He tormented the librarian, Father Hubert, with constant absurd demands. "The excellent bureaucrat," wrote Verlaine, "whose very functions obliged him to deliver to Rimbaud, at the latter's request, a great many Oriental tales and libretti of Favari, together with vague scientific booklets, very old and very rare, used to rage at having to get up for this urchin, and preferred to send him, orally, to his own favorite studies, to Cicero, to Horace, and to goodness knows what Greeks besides." Rimbaud remained unmoved. Churlish, with his eternally wicked smile and his air of bravado, he persisted in asking for "works whose very names were disagreeable to the

73

ears of the librarian." There were altercations, consequently, and even strong language passed between them. Father Hubert was not accommodating; even Louis Pierquin was once literally kicked out for having asked for the *Contes* of La Fontaine. Rimbaud used to plunge ostentatiously, and to the great horror of the habitués, into the works of Helvetius and Jean-Jacques Rousseau, into treatises on sorcery, cabalism and alchemy. "Why did he need all those heretical conjuring books?" The future Pilgrim of Hell worried not at all about these mutterings. They could grumble all they wanted around him. He took his revenge in verse on his critics. In a poem written in January, 1871 (*les Assis*), he describes them maliciously, "dark in their spectacles . . . their fists clenched within their dirty cuffs."

Poor little old men! They breathe a sigh of relief when they see the trouble-maker leave the room. No sooner does he slam the door irritably than they adjust their spectacles and begin again to turn the leaves of their favorite gazettes, magazines and almanacs. But one day he bursts in with nasty glee: "Paris has surrendered!" The news fills his hearers with consternation but delights Rimbaud. At last the doors of destiny are opening for him. He was not made to live in this timorous city, in this sordid and dusty library. He is intoxicated with pride. He is elated at the thought that he is not like other men.

Later he wrote: "I am the saint praying on the terrace, like animals grazing on the banks of the Palestinian sea.

"I am the scientist in his somber armchair. Branches of trees and raindrops hurl themselves against the casement windows of the library.

"I am the pedestrian on the broad highway through the dwarf woods; the murmuring of the water over the dams covers my steps. I look long at the melancholy golden soap-suds of the setting sun.

"I should like to be a child left on a jetty that is cut off by the tide, or a little page walking up an avenue whose summit touches the sky.

"The paths are bitter. The hillocks are covered with furze. The air is motionless. How far away are the birds and the spring? It can only be the end of the world ahead of me!"

Yes, the end of the world. . . . Advance, advance always. Now begins the great adventure. His is to be "free liberty." His, perhaps—who knows?—glory.

But first he must set off to Paris. The great city fascinates him. Three times in succession, he is destined to make the longed-for journey.

IV

THE CALL OF PARIS

THE pettiness of life in the provinces fills Rimbaud with revulsion. He is disheartened and nauseated. Yonder by the abandoned bivouacs, with her suburbs still smoking from the last battles of the siege, Paris beckons him.

The summer before he had barely had a glimpse of the city through the barred windows of the Mazas prison, and the great unknown world attracted him irresistibly, more tempting, more disturbing than before in the desolation of defeat and the uncertainty of destiny.

The world has become plastic: everything is changing, seething, everything is in the melting pot. Make way for the strong, for those who pride themselves on being heartless and who know how to carve out careers for themselves on a heroic scale! He leaves.

He takes advantage of the first re-establishment of communications with the capital—this takes place on February 25, 1871—and as he has little money, he sells his watch to pay for his ticket. This time he is not alone. The "heartless one" is accompanied by a young girl from Charleville who leaves her home and family to go with him. Ernest Delahaye tells the story—"As they had no place to go the first night, they slept on a boulevard bench. In the morning he insisted on her quitting him, on her taking the few sous left to them both and returning to the Gare du Nord. He hoped that she would be taken in by some relatives in a little town near Paris." [1]

The recollections of M. Louis Pierquin confirm the tale of Ernest Delahaye. She who came to Paris with Rimbaud was the girl of violet eyes sung in the sonnet *Voyelles*. Aside from this one thing that we know of her, she is a creature of mystery, a fugitive shadow impossible to grasp, to seize in passage. Who was she? What became of her? The silence of her lover has shielded her secret. "Rimbaud," says M. Louis Pierquin, "did not like any one to refer to this brief and painful love-affair. Several years later I was sitting with him one evening at the Café Duterme, rue du Petit-Bois, in Charleville, a café not much frequented except on Sundays. That evening he was silent, hardly bothering to answer my questions. I felt that his mind was working over some painful subject. To divert him, I said: 'Well, what has happened to your love-affair? Have you any news of the little girl?' He fixed his eyes upon mine with an expression of profound misery, and an-

[1] M. Marcel Coulon does not give credence to this story of a double flight. In fact, it would interfere with his theory of the relations between Verlaine and Rimbaud. As for Paterne Berrichon, self-appointed defender of Rimbaud's chastity, he passes over the incident in silence.

swered: 'I beg of you, don't speak of it!' He spread his elbows on the table, put his head in his hands, and burst into tears. I shall never forget that heart-rending scene. Toward nine o'clock he got up, saying: 'Let's go!' I accompanied him to the gate of the forest of La Havetière, about a mile from the town. He pressed my hand without a word, still suppressing a sob, then took a path across the woods. I did not see him again for five days.

"A short time after his death, in a conversation I had with his sister Isabelle, I told her these facts, of which she had been ignorant. 'What you are telling me,' she said, 'explains certain incoherent words that he repeated frequently during his delirium.' "

The last memory of the secret love-affair was revived on his death-bed.

When his little friend had left him—for his devotion to literature demanded this sacrifice—Rimbaud went about the streets alone, bent on the conquest of Paris. Bewildered at first by the noise and activity of the great city, he loitered under the galleries of the Odéon, wandered aimlessly along the boulevards, then turned up at the home of the good-natured caricaturist André Gill, whose address he had obtained somewhere.

He arrives at the door. It is open. There is no one in the studio. He enters, with his usual air of confidence, and does just as he did at the Givet barracks, when the sergeant was away, and at Douai at the home of his teacher Izambard: he spies a couch, lies down, and goes to sleep. In the evening André Gill, returning, is amazed to find an unknown person sleeping in his room.

"Say there! Who are you? What are you doing there?"

"I am Arthur Rimbaud," says the poet, sitting up and rubbing his eyes. "You were wrong to wake me up; I was just having the most beautiful dreams!"

"I have them too," answers Gill, "but I have them in my own bed!" and he sends the boy away, gently, however, giving him all the money in his pocket—a ten-franc piece—and some good advice.

And now what is there for him to do in this city exhausted by the horrors of the siege, without a lodging, without a place to warm himself, soon even without bread, in the biting wintry weather. Rimbaud wanders about aimlessly for two weeks, shivering before the windows of book-shops, sleeping under the bridges or on coal-barges, and finally, indignant at a Paris that will not take him in, he sets out again on foot for the Ardennes, March 10th, 1871.

The countryside was still infested with Germans. Should he try to convince the peasants, vaguely disquieted by his strange appearance, of his true identity, he would only arouse more suspicion. Dependent as he was on their good will for food and shelter, he decided to pass himself off as a franc-tireur hiding from the enemy. The ruse worked.

He arrived home one night, his clothing in shreds, coughing as if he were about to give up the ghost.

79

His mother took care of him, clothed him anew, and read him a sermon. "Come," she said. "It's time you began to take things seriously. You've had enough of these wild notions!" She would have liked him to re-enter college. Let him at least finish his studies and try for a degree—like everybody else!

She is only wasting her time. At this moment she can make little headway with such advice! He is in conflict with society and is working on the plan of a constitution for a communist state, inspired by Jean-Jacques and Babeuf.[1] He spends his time proselytising the stone-breakers along the highroad, preaching the Social Revolution. Heavens, what would he be doing at college? He is much more comfortable with Delahaye, "among the birch trees and the laburnum and the young groves of locust, all gray and pink, studded with gold and emerald," or even in the depths of an old stone-quarry cut into the side of the Saint Laurent Hill.

Once more he thinks he sees his great chance beckoning him from the heart of war-torn Paris. Is this his fortune at last, the fortune that had failed to smile on him in literature? The red glow of the Commune flickers in the depths of his dreams and dazzles him. Now again, for the third time in eight months, he sets out for Paris, on foot, naturally, and without a cent in his pocket. But he is now at home along the open road. If a cart passes he does not hesitate to call out to the driver and ask for a "lift."

[1] The notebook containing this plan, written out in a fine hand, was shown to Delahaye in August, 1871, and has not been found since.

These are always a few leagues gained. He pays for the ride by telling stories.

One day a tipsy driver who had just given him passage between some sacks of wheat and a load of casks demanded in payment "a picture for his boy." He persisted, drunkenly, in his demand, and so to get rid of him Rimbaud tore a page out of his notebook and drew him a caricature of M. Thiers.

Did he really reach Paris this time? Did he join the insurgents? Was he an incendiary and a communist soldier as he boasted he was? This version has been accepted up to the present by all his biographers, and the various incidents are well known. He presents himself at the fortifications as a recruit from the provinces and demands arms. To be sure, he is only a child to the hardy communist troops, but his strange expression and his passionate arguments win their confidence; they take up a collection for him and he entertains them in return. Exchange of favors. Then the situation of the insurgents becomes more precarious, and Rimbaud is enrolled in the "sharpshooters of the Revolution." But at the Babylon barracks, where he is quartered, he receives neither arms nor equipment. The Versaillais (Thierists) approach the city, and he has to flee for his life in the general disorder. The famous triolets of the *Cœur volé* are supposed to have been inspired by his disheartening experiences in the canteens of the revolutionists.

Although it seems very prosaic, we must consider this tale with a great deal of scepticism. In the first

81

place, Rimbaud's poem of the *Cœur volé* was written before his departure for the Communes and was sent to M. Izambard in a letter from Charleville dated May 13, 1871. "I am going to be a workman," he wrote in the letter accompanying the poem. "This is what holds me back when madness and anger urge me toward the battle of Paris where so many workmen are dying even while I write to you." Thus he is far from the Babylon Barracks at this date and cannot write a description of it.

Furthermore, he is still in Charleville on the 15th of May. We have proof of this in a famous letter addressed on that very day to his friend Paul Demeny at Douai. We are forced, then, to place his experience of the Communes between the 16th and the 20th of May, at the beginning of the Versailles repressions and of "bloody week," but, if we allow him a week to go to the capital from the Ardennes (a distance of 240 kilometers), we must conclude that he hardly could have had time to "burn up" Paris, or even to enroll himself among the incendiaries.

However, it is quite possible that he actually set forth, as we have no reason to doubt the episode of the forest of Villers-Cotterets, so often told. One night, by the light of a Raffet moon, as Verlaine says, he escaped miraculously from a patrol of Uhlans by throwing himself, trembling with fear, into a thicket, the clang of arms and the thunder of horses' hooves ringing in his ears. He experienced the same fatigues, the same miseries, the same dangers as on his other trips home. And when he arrived in Charleville he was more enervated, more embittered than ever.

He has thus far been baffled in his talents, which no one has recognized, in his revolutionary ardor, which has been thwarted; there is one more humiliation in store for him—that of his manly pride. He plans a little romance with the daughter of a Charleville manufacturer—a neighbor—which results only in ridicule and confusion. At the end of May, 1871, while in the act of leaving his own home, he perceived, behind the curtained window of a house on the Quai de la Madeleine, a brunette with blue eyes "above all praise." She seemed very attractive. He sent her verses—a lyric declaration of love— and with that awkward candor which overcame at moments his exaggerated cynicism, he arranged a meeting with her at the Square de la Gare. The beauty appeared, accompanied by a sly duenna who was her accomplice, measured the big, timid booby, ill-clad, shy, "as scared as thirty-six million new-born poodle-dogs," and then walked on, mocking, with a contemptuous smile. Obviously the young poet made no favorable impression on the little bourgeoise.

His revolt was now directed against everything. It was during this summer that he wrote the invective *Mes petites amoureuses* and most of his cynical and irreligious poems; *les Accroupissements, les Pauvres à l'Eglise, les Premières Communions.* In *Paris se repeuple,* he bursts into fury against the riot squads, against the government of Thiers, against woman also, eternal accomplice of the middle classes swollen with gold.

> *Société! Tout est rétabli: les orgies*
> *Pleurent leur ancien râle aux anciens lupanars. . . .*

> Society! All is healed again: the orgies
> Scream as of old from the old bawdy-houses. . . .

His irritability frightens his mother and his sisters; his coarseness, his bravado and turbulence offend the good citizens of Charleville. The boys of the neighborhood, seeing him pass, take note of his insolent air, his soiled clothes, his long hair hanging in ringlets over his shoulders, his pipe with its bowl upside down and half falling from his mouth; they point him out to each other and throw stones at him, trying to infuriate him.

One day, on the Place Ducale, he is addressed by a young clerk who tries to insult him by offering him a nickel: "Here, little man, take this and get yourself a haircut." Rimbaud, stronger-minded than the joker, puts the money into his pocket without batting an eyelash. "This will do," he says, "to buy me some tobacco." Above all he arouses the indignation of the local tobacconist, a severe old woman with an eagle eye and a hooked nose, by entering her shop—his short-pipe between his teeth, his cap stuck on the side of his head, and demanding in an imperious tone: "A penny's worth of pipe tobacco!" And from time to time, for diversion, he writes in

84

chalk in large capitals on the public benches or on the doors of churches, "Death to God!"

What room could there be in his ungovernable soul for any kind of compromise, with religion, society, or literature? He tries not to be in accord with his time, but to go beyond it, to anticipate it, to be a prophet or a seer.

In two characteristic letters, written at an interval of two days, one May 13, 1871, to M. Izambard, the other, on the 15th, to Paul Demeny, he explains his theory of the new poetry and his conception of the rôle of the poet-seer. The first has not yet been published (M. Izambard intends to publish it later). The second, more complete, very ironical, full of obscurity shot through with light, has already been published.

Nothing has existed in poetry, says Rimbaud in this letter, since the time of Ancient Greece. Nothing except centuries of versification. "The man who wishes to become a poet must first apply himself to complete self-knowledge. He searches for his soul, he examines it, tries it, learns to know it. As soon as he does know it, he must cultivate it. This seems simple enough: in every brain a natural development takes place; so many *egoists* call themselves authors; and there are a great many others who attribute their intellectual progress to themselves!—But the real problem is to make the soul monstrous: in imitation of comprachicos or their like! It is as if a man were to plant and cultivate warts on his face.

85

"I say that we must become *seers*, we must make ourselves seers. The poet makes himself a seer by a long, immense, deliberate derangement of all the senses. All the forms of love, pain, madness; he seeks in himself, he exhausts all the poisons within himself and retains only their quintessence. Ineffable torment in which he has need of all possible faith, all possible superhuman strength, in which he becomes among all men the great sick man, the great criminal, the great accursed one—and the supreme savant. For he reaches the unknown! since he has cultivated his already fertile imagination more than any one else. He reaches the unknown; and if maddened, he should end by losing understanding of his visions, at least he has seen them! Let him burst with his straining after unheard of and unnameable things; there will come other horrible workers who will begin at the very horizons in sight of which he expired."

Then follows a curious page of literary history: "Lamartine is sometimes a seer, but strangled by the old forms. Hugo, *too headstrong*, must certainly have *seen* in his later volumes: *les Miserables* is a true poem. . . . Musset is execrable to the nth degree for our generations in the painful grip of visions —whom his angelic indolence has insulted. Oh what insipid tales and proverbs! O *les Nuits*, O *Namouna*, O *la Coupe!* They are all French, that is to say supreme, detestable, French, not Parisian! Still another product of that evil genius that moved Rabelais, Voltaire, Jean la Fontaine, and was commented on by M. Taine! How vernal is Musset's spirit! How charming his loves! Here we have fine enamel work —solid poetry! *French* poetry will be enjoyed for a long time, but only in France. Every grocer's boy is capable of reeling off a Rollaësque apostrophe, every seminary scholar carries a little rhyming dictionary around with him secretly. . . .

"The secondary romantics are great seers; Théophile Gautier, Leconte de Lisle, Théodore de Banville. But since examining the invisible and listening to the inaudible are different from regaining the spirit of dead things, Baudelaire is the first of all seers, king of poets, a *true god!* But even he lived in too artistic a milieu, and the form on which he prides himself so, is paltry. The inventions of the unknown require new forms."

Let the old forms disappear! If he has used them himself, he regrets it, he is ashamed of them. And so he is perfectly consistent with himself when he writes a month later to Paul Demeny:

"I beg of you, and I believe that you will respect my wish as if it came from the dead, burn all the verses that I was stupid enough to give you when I was staying at Douai." He is working now toward the realization of his poetic ideal: he is about to write: *Ce qu'on dit au poète à propos de fleurs* and *le Bateau ivre.*

It is well known how few writers of his time found favor in his eyes: of these two poems, he sends one to Théodore de Banville and carries the other to

87

Verlaine. On July 14, 1871, he writes to Banville:
"Do you remember having received from the prov-
inces in June, 1870, one hundred or one hundred and
fifty hexameters on a mythical subject entitled
Credo in unam? (This is the poem published under
the title of *Soleil et chair.*) You were good enough to
answer. The same imbecile sends you the enclosed
verses." "The enclosed verses," *Ce qu'on dit au poète
à propos de fleurs*, were published in 1925 by M.
Marcel Coulon. They are acrobatic fantasies in which
Rimbaud, with prodigious verbal originality, gives
rein to all his profane ingenuity. M. Coulon has com-
pared it, logically, to the *Bateau ivre;* it is, on the
comic plane, what the other poem is on a "sublime
plane." It is the same flight of the imagination into
exoticism. Rimbaud abandons the common French
plants, crabbed, sickly and pitiful, for those un-
known, unheard of, inexistent flora of the tropics and
the Floridas of his impossible dreams. But at the
same time that he tears the petals of the detested
roses, lilies, violets, forget-me-nots—detested because
he has them, because they exist, and since that which
he has not, which he cannot have, and which does not
exist is so obviously what he most desires—he con-
demns his own stupidity, his own absurdity. Mock-
ingly he jeers at himself, addresses himself ironically:

> *Sers-nous, ô farceur, tu le peux,*
> *Sur un plat de vermeil splendide*
> *Des ragoûts de lys sirupeux*
> *Mordant nos cuillers d'alfénide!*

> Serve us, o clown, as thou canst
> Upon a splendid vermillion plate
> Ragouts of syropy lilies—
> We who lick our German-silver spoons.

And at the end:

> *Surtout rime une version*
> *Sur le mal des pommes de terre.* . . .
>
> By all means, let us make some rhymes
> On the potato disease. . . .

Ah! eternal sarcasm, thwarted enthusiasm, flight that subsides always in self-derision, lassitude, nausea. He will never be satisfied, and under his weary glance all flowers fade, all stars pale!

Toward the end of August, 1871, before ever having seen the sea, he wrote the poem which, perhaps more than anything else he has done, has made him famous: *le Bateau ivre.* In this we find the same daring, the same incoherence, the same richness. Resolved as he was to break with the old formulas, the traditional procedure of literary notation which had fixed and worn out the changing and elusive sensuous world, aspiring to renew the value of words which he finds impoverished, he asserts his violently personal idiom with amazing virtuosity for a youth of sixteen. For logical sequences of trite images, he substitutes a perfect tempest of new verbal combinations. Out of his schoolboy reading: *Twenty-Thousand Leagues under the Sea,* and *Toilers of the Sea,* he creates a marvelous vision. His poem swells like

89

a free tide as he prophesies his own legendary and pathetic destiny in an ever richer and ever unfolding symbolism: to see all, to feel all, to exhaust everything, to explore everything, to say everything. His passionate, savage curiosity carries him away toward the unknown, the invisible, the unutterable.

Je sais les cieux crevant en éclairs, et les trombes,
Et les ressacs, et les courants; je sais le soir,
L'aube exaltée ainsi qu'un peuple de colombes,
Et j' ai vu quelquefois ce que l'homme a cru voir. . . .

J'ai rêvé la nuit verte aux neiges éblouies,
Baisers montant aux yeux des mers avec lenteur,
La circulation des sèves inouies,
Et l'éveil jaune et bleu des phosphores chanteurs.

I know the skies bursting in lightning, I know
The whirlpools, the tides, the seas, I know the evenings,
The transfigured dawn like a throng of doves,
And I have sometimes seen that which man hoped to
see. . . .

Here is the bottom of the sea:

I have dreamed of nights green with luminous snow,
The kisses rising slowly to the eyes of the sea,
Of the steady circulating of incredible saps,
And the yellow and blue waking of singing phosphorus.

The pilotless ship, carried along, drifting, in the intoxication of ideal meditations, has seen everything: great battles of the waves, unknown cataracts, unique visions never the same and never seen by other beholders:

90

Glaciers, soleils d'argent, flots nacreux, cieux de braises
Echouages hideux au fond des golfes bruns.

Glaciers, silver suns and pearly floods,
Molten skies and hideous stranding places
In the depths of brown gulfs.

It has been bathed "in the poem of the sea infused with stars," where "goldfish pass through the flowery foam." Like the poet himself, "a mad plank accompanied by black sea horses," it has sailed all the seas of ideas and images. It has been "the eternal truant of the blind infinite," and now it is weary. Rimbaud ends here on a note of complete nihilism:

Mais vrai, j'ai trop pleuré. Les aubes sont navrantes,
Toute lune est atroce et tout soleil amer.
L'âcre amour m'a gonflé de torpeurs enivrantes
Oh! que ma quille éclate! Oh! que j'aille à la mer!

But in truth, I have wept too much. The grey dawns
Break the heart, each moon is hateful; and each sun
  embitters.
An acrid love has filled me with a poisonous languor.
Oh! let my keel burst! Oh let me go to the sea!

To whom can one read such verses when one is sixteen and one lives in Charleville? It certainly is not easy to find a public. "It is more than a year," he writes in August to Paul Demeny, "since I have left the common life for the type of life you know (the life of a 'seer'). Forever locked up within this indescribable Ardennes country, seeing no one, withdrawn as I am into this infamous, silly, obstinate,

91

mysterious labor, answering questions and vulgar and wicked reproaches only with silence, bearing myself worthily in my extra-legal position, I have finally brought down on myself the most horrible condemnations from a mother who is as inflexible as sixty-three helmeted administrations. She wanted to condemn me to perpetual hard labor in Charleville (Ardennes). Get yourself a job by such and such a date, or get out, she said. I refused to give my reasons: it would have been useless. Up to now I have been able to postpone the fatal day. She has come to the point where she longs continually to have me leave, run away. Penniless and inexperienced, I shall end, she says, by entering a house of correction. And from that time on, nothing will be heard of me . . ." And he adds: "I am willing to work hard, but in Paris, which I love."

In his desire to regain the capital, Rimbaud darkens the picture of his intellectual distress. He is not as lonely as he says, and frequents, without too great suffering, a few school and café friends besides the faithful Delahaye: Ernest Millot, Louis Pierquin, the teacher Lenel, and above all two jolly companions of "advanced" tendencies who are frightened neither by his poetry nor his external disarray: Bretagne and Deverrière.

Bretagne was a "cellar-rat," athletic and pot-bellied, a great pipe-smoker and a Bohemian by choice, who knew Verlaine and prided himself on his interest in literature. He resembled a debonair Henry the Eighth or the drinker in Manet's *Bon bock.* He was a musician as well, an excellent violinist, and had a talent for caricature which he exercised with a lively and biting facility. Deverrière was a jovial fat fellow, a bearded radical, and a great reader of Helvetius. He had been a teacher, and was at this time an editor of the *Nord-Est*, the republican newspaper of the Ardennes.

The three friends were often to be found seated at a table in a café on the Place Ducale, under the arcades, arguing over their foaming beer in the clouded air of the smoking room. Stroking his black beard, Bretagne told of his meeting with Verlaine in Artois. There was none more kindly than the author of the *Fêtes Galantes.* Since Rimbaud wanted to go to Paris to make a name for himself, why didn't he write to Verlaine? Stimulated by this suggestion, Rimbaud had Delahaye copy over his latest poems in a round hand and joined to this specimen of penmanship "a long letter in fine writing in which he told his ideals, his passions, his enthusiasms, his weariness, all that he was." Bretagne ended the communication with an affectionate postscript, and two weeks later Verlaine, enraptured by these strange and novel accents, invited the author of the *Bateau ivre* to come to Paris.

V

THE TEMPLE OF THE MUSES

T HE evening before his departure," Ernest De-
lahaye relates, "Rimbaud wanted to take a
last walk about the environs of Charleville. This
was in December, 1871. The sun was bright and mild,
the air delicate, delightfully warm, everything
seemed hopeful. We sat down at the edge of a wood:
'This,' he said, 'is what I have prepared to show
them when I arrive.' And he read me the *Bateau ivre*.
Upon hearing this truly astonishing work, I an-
nounced in advance the thunderous entry that he
would make thereby into the world of letters. 'Ah,
yes,' he answered, 'no one has ever written anything
like it. I know indeed. And yet? The world of lit-
erary men, of artists! The salons! The elegancies!
I don't even know how to carry myself. I am awk-
ward, timid, I don't know how to talk. Oh, so far as
ideas are concerned I'm not afraid of anybody, but
. . . Ah, what am I going to do there?' "

This time his departure was serious: he was going
to stake out his career. He was leaving, no longer as
a vagabond, but as a traveler. His mother, despair-

ing of ever being able to turn him into a clerk of steady habits, was not averse to letting him go, and true to her custom, gave him no money but bought him a new suit. Deverrière gave him twenty francs to pay for his ticket.

He bade adieu, then, to Charleville, to the lively Meuse shimmering under the arch of the Vieux-Moulin, to the ramparts of Mézières, moss-grown and bathed in green water, to the cafés of the Place Ducale, nestling like caves under the arcades of the tall Louis XIII pavilions with their slippery blue roofs.

In the golden haze through which his train slid toward Paris at twilight, he could see arising the porticoes and pediments of the Temple of the Muses on the Acropolis of his dreams!

"Come, dear, great soul, we await you, we want you," Verlaine had written. To tell the truth, it was not in his own home, but in the home of his wife's parents, at 14 rue Nicolet, up on Montmartre, that he offered this hospitality. The year before he had married little Mlle. Mathilde Mauté, daughter of a retired Norman notary. The honeymoon was short. The *Bonne Chanson*, his Epithalamion, was quickly forgotten in the tumult of the war. Soon after came the horrors of the siege of Paris, the irregular life under the National Guard, drinking parties on the ramparts, the prostration attending the Communes. The young wife was weary of scenes of drunkenness, of cursing and brutality.

And now her husband inflicted on her the presence of a stranger with very disagreeable manners, in her father's home, and in her father's absence.

Verlaine himself had been surprised. He was expecting to see a man of about thirty—in fact, he did not recognize Rimbaud at the station and only found him an hour after the arrival of the train comfortably installed at the rue Nicolet. At this time Rimbaud was a very thin, coarse-looking urchin, a tall, ill-formed peasant lad with great red hands, extremely awkward. "A round, fresh child's head," Verlaine wrote later, "on a big bony body, ungainly as that of a still growing adolescent." He had an Ardennes accent, a very provincial air, and, as Mallarmé said, "a kind of pride in his vulgar extraction." However, he attracted people by the gracious oval of his face, and his eyes "like a summer night," those steely eyes flecked with golden light, the blue iris set in a darker ring, those "cruel" eyes in which there glowed and smiled nevertheless a sort of gentleness. His skin was tanned; under his light brown hair, always disordered, his expression had hardened. His mouth, strong, sensual, red, had a bitter, cunning line.

The first dinner at the rue Nicolet was frightful. There were present Mme. Mauté, Verlaine's mother-in-law, his wife, who was eight months gone with child and somewhat poor in health, and Charles Cros, the poet-physicist, invited for the occasion. M. Mauté was away from home. The company sat down at table without enthusiasm. Rimbaud ate greedily, his nose in his plate, without saying a

96

word, occasionally throwing a hostile and mistrustful glance about him. By now he too was disappointed. The two women put themselves out to make conversation: was he tired? had he had a pleasant trip? Rimbaud barely opened his lips, answered their questions wearily. Then Charles Cros spoke to him about his poetry. Insolent and stubborn silence was his only response. He put his elbows on the table, lit his pipe, drew a few puffs, then got up and went to bed.

One can imagine what comments were exchanged afterwards by the assembled company. "He isn't amusing, that fellow! . . . and then . . . such total lack of good manners. . . . Father will not tolerate him for a moment when he returns, etc." Verlaine tried hard to defend him a little, but the next day and the days after things went from bad to worse. Rimbaud became more and more irritated by this bourgeois atmosphere that differed so little from that of his own home. He found the same taste and manners as in Charleville, the same Louis Philippe furniture, the same round table and clock as in his mother's house, the faded crayon-portrait of the grandfather in the bedroom. A poet, to his mind, should live otherwise. He said this crudely to Verlaine, who asked nothing better than to be persuaded to escape from the restrictions of his domestic life, to regain his liberty. Rimbaud drew him into long drinking parties on the café terraces. They could be seen every day going down the hill of Montmartre and crossing over to the left bank, swinging between

97

the Café de Cluny and the Café Tabourey, near the Odéon, where they would meet questionable literary personages. It was always very late before they tore themselves away from the Latin Quarter and climbed up to Montmartre again. They often returned drunk: whereupon there would be fresh family rows between Verlaine and his wife. M. Mauté announced his imminent return, and they greatly feared his sharp temper. Could they continue living this way? Fortunately, at the end of two weeks, Rimbaud took himself off.

What became of him then? No one knows. Verlaine met him one day, wandering alone along the streets, emaciated, half-dead with hunger, his clothes dirty and torn, and went to plead for him before the good master Théodore de Banville. Banville responded nobly, and rented a student's room in the rue de Buci for the vagabond. Mme. de Banville helped by sending a bed up to the bare little garret. Rimbaud accepted the arrangements of his friends, but no sooner had he arrived in the room than he provoked a scandal. He had been sleeping for days in some cheap lodging and had come out of it quite covered with vermin. Now he undressed himself quickly, took off his filthy shirt, and going to the window quite naked, threw it into the street. Complaints were made by the outraged neighbors; explanations followed. "But I couldn't lie down to sleep in such a clean bed," he said to Banville, "with my clothes full of lice!"

A few days later, anyway, he moved again. The

bed lent by Mme. de Banville was carried to the laboratory where Charles Cros was living with the painter Michel de l'Hay. Next the musician Cabaner —he whom Verlaine so delightfully named "Jesus Christ after three-years-of-absinthe,"—took him home to his place in the rue Racine. Finally, as he wished to be by himself, his protectors banded themselves together and assessed themselves to assure him a small income . . . of three francs a day. He was installed, with a few wretched pieces of furniture, in a garret in the rue Campagne-Première, at a yearly rental of twenty-five francs a year.[1] He remained there three months, from January to April, 1872, and it was at this time that he made the acquaintance of Forain.

Verlaine was becoming more and more enthusiastic about Rimbaud. For him Rimbaud emerged from his long silences. What a companion he was! His intelligence, his novel attitudes fascinated Verlaine. But whenever he took the boy to meet his friends, or to literary gatherings, he was a source of disappointment, unpleasantness, mortification.

Savage, awkward, cynical, certainly the "infant prodigy" had all appearances against him. With his crude shyness and his frightful obstinacy, he could not or would not adapt himself either to the social proprieties or to the elementary rules of literary courtesy. He respected nothing and nobody.

One day Verlaine's friend and biographer, Ed-

---

[1] At times when his income was not forthcoming, or inadequate, Rimbaud used to peddle key-rings under the arcades in the Rue de Rivoli, or work as a waiter in a Montmartre café.—*Tr.*

mond Lepelletier, invited the two poets to dinner. Rimbaud was unbearable. "In the first place," wrote his host, "he didn't open his mouth to speak during the whole first part of the meal, except to ask for bread or something to drink, and this in a dry tone, as if he were in a restaurant. Then, at the end, under the influence of a strong Burgundy wine which Verlaine served him generously, he became aggressive. He shot off a volley of paradoxes and sweeping generalizations. He tried especially to tease me by calling me 'greeter of the dead' because he had often seen me lifting my hat to a passing funeral procession. As I had just lost my mother two months before, I forbade him to go on at this rate, and looked at him so severely that he took umbrage and tried to approach me menacingly. He had, nervously and stupidly, taken hold of a dessert knife, as a weapon, no doubt. I clapped my hand on his shoulder and forced him to sit down immediately, assuring him, that since I had not been afraid of the Prussians, I was not likely to be intimidated by a mischievous child like him. I added, without great anger, somewhat jokingly, that if he weren't satisfied and insisted on annoying us, I would send him downstairs with a few good kicks in the lower part of the back. Verlaine interposed, begging me not to be angry, and apologized for his friend. Rimbaud was silent until the end of the meal, contenting himself with drinking a liberal quantity of wine and surrounding himself with clouds of smoke, while Verlaine recited poetry."

100

Verlaine was not discouraged despite the recurrence of such incidents. He was proud of his protégé and wanted to exhibit him everywhere. He introduced him to the various literary coteries and brought him to see Victor Hugo. If the old poet did not greet him, as has been claimed, with the appellation of "infant Shakespeare"—this title seems to have been addressed to Glatigny—at least he did receive him with his usual Olympian benevolence and facile rhetoric. Fantin-Latour obtained a single sitting from Rimbaud—in the course of which "the subject" did not deign to speak a single word—and placed him, such as he saw him, leaning on his elbow like a sulky and disagreeable schoolboy in his famous painting *le Coin de table,* along with Léon Valade, Emile Blémont, Verlaine, Jean Aicard and Camille Pelletan.

In November, 1871, Verlaine brought Ernest Delahaye to visit Rimbaud at the Hotel des Etrangers in the rue Racine. They found him in a filthy salon presided over by Cabaner in the midst of men of letters and esthetes, duly long-haired and bearded. "The first thing I saw," wrote Delahaye, "was Rimbaud, who had been lying on a divan, getting up as we came in, stretching, rubbing his eyes, making the pitiable grimaces of a child suddenly wakened from a sound sleep. Standing up, erect, he seemed huge to me. . . . He had grown more than a foot in a few weeks." "One saw no more the round cheeks of other times. On these elongated, bony features, the high color of a cabman burned dreadfully around his

101

blue eyes." He was disheveled and dirty, clothed in a long raincoat, fearfully crumpled and twice too long for him, his head covered with a greasy felt hat that was faded and out of shape. "He explained to us that he had just taken some hashish and had thrown himself down just as he was, so as to have the delicious visions that had been promised him. But he had been completely disappointed. He had seen white moons and black moons pursuing each other at varying rates of speed, and that was all . . . except for an upset stomach and a frightful headache. I advised him to go out for some air. We took a long walk along the boulevard and around the Panthéon. He showed me the mutilated columns. 'The work of cannon-balls,' he said. Everywhere, along the way, one could see similar marks on the buildings. I asked him about the new ideas in Paris. In a tired voice he answered a few short words which revealed a collapse of all hope, 'Nothing, chaos, all kinds of reaction possible and even probable.' "

In spite of the efforts of Verlaine, Rimbaud had no success in Paris. The Temple of the Muses remained closed to him. His poems seemed a challenge to poetry, his attitude a challenge to the literary fellowship. "A passer-by of importance," Mallarmé said of him. In reality, he was a mysterious and annoying passer-by. One evening, at the dinner of the "Vilains Bonhommes," which brought together at the café of the Théatre Bobino in the rue Madame, writers like Banville, Hérédia, Coppée, a quarrel arose between Rimbaud and the photographer Carjat. The "kid," who was quite drunk, systematically interrupted one of those present (Jean Aicard, supposedly, who was reading one of his poems) with the word of Cambronne. "Snot-nose," cried Carjat, thoroughly incensed, "if you don't keep quiet I'll box your ears!" In answer, Rimbaud seized Verlaine's sword-cane, lunged toward his adversary, and wounded him slightly. There was a general hue and cry. The painter Michel de l'Hay disarmed the boy, and led him back only half sobered up, to his room in the rue Campagne-Première. It was decided to exclude him thenceforth from these love-feasts.

He had come to Paris to seek literary acclaim; but little by little, he was succeeding only in alienating all the literary men. Despite Verlaine's growing attachment—a fact which was already causing tongues to wag—Rimbaud suddenly left the capital in April, 1872.

This sojourn of six months was not without profit for him. By coming into headlong conflict with the reigning esthete of the Parnassian school, he became even more conscious of his own originality. He had no use for anthology "pieces," the ingeniously arranged compositions of a Leconte de Lisle or a Hérédia. With savage joy the iconoclast in him mutilated the bas-reliefs of the Temple of the Muses. He was, according to the phrase of Ernest Delahaye, a sensationist. He was eternally looking for sensations, transmutations, distortions.

He felt more strongly than ever the need for reconciling music and painting, the art of design and the art of rhythm, the need for discovering a poetic language that would engage all the senses at once, which would be "of the soul, for the soul," which would include "everything, perfume, sound, color," as he had written to his friend Paul Demeny. He could have used, as an inscription to his musical painting: *les Chercheuses de Poux*, that famous line of Baudelaire's: "Perfumes, colors and sounds correspond."

The initial impression that gave birth to this lovely poem may have been the garret in the rue de Buci where he shook off his own vermin so as to spare Mme. de Banville's clean bed-linen. But what a rare and delicate transposition he made, what harmonious polychromy!

Quand le front de l'enfant plein de rouges tourmentes
Implore l'essaim blanc des rêves indistincts,
Il vient près de son lit deux grandes soeurs charmantes
Avec de frêles doigts aux ongles argentins.

Elles assoient l'enfant auprès d'une croisée
Grande ouverte où l'air bleu baigne un fouillis de fleurs
Et dans ses lourds cheveux où tombe la rosée
Promènent leurs doigts fins, terribles et charmeurs.

Il écoute chanter leurs haleines craintives
Qui fleurent de longs miels végétaux et roses
Et qu'interrompt parfois un sifflement, salives
Reprises sur la lèvre ou désirs de baisers.

Il entend leurs cils noirs battant sous les silences
Parfumés, et leurs doigts électriques et doux
Font crépiter, parmi ses grises indolences,
Sous leurs ongles royaux la mort des petits poux.

Voilà que monte en lui le Vin de la Paresse,
Soupir d'harmonica qui pourrait délirer:
L'enfant se sent, selon la lenteur des caresses,
Sourdre et mourir sans cesse un désir de pleurer.[1]

At about the same time Rimbaud wrote the *Quatrain* and the celebrated "Sonnet of the Vowels," inspired, it is believed, by the memory of a childhood primer, and in which certain Symbolists have detected a code of verbal instrumentation.

A noir, E blanc, I rouge, U vert, O bleu, voyelles,
Je dirai quelque jour vos naissances latentes. . . .[2]

Rimbaud is enamoured of new sensations, of unusual images, and he seeks them, if need be, in drunkenness, in the excitement of alcohol or of hashish, in the smoke of tobacco. He labors to discover new rhythms, and his inventions in prosody will lead him to freer and freer forms until he works into the prose of the *Illuminations* and of the *Saison en enfer*.

It is a matter of common knowledge what influence this audacious esthetics exercised over Verlaine. With the *Bonne Chanson*, Verlaine had already begun to separate himself from the Parnassian ideal. The ice of the *Poèmes saturniens* had melted, the crystalline water had escaped and spread its gushing melody everywhere, variable and sinuous. After contact with Rimbaud's ideas, Verlaine gave his poetry a more personal, and, if I may say so, a still more arbitrary accent. His technique became

[1] NOTE: See translation by T. Sturge Moore in the Appendix.
[2] NOTE: See translation by Joseph T. Shipley in the Appendix.

105

more supple, and, in the *Romances sans Paroles*, he put into practice the precept expressed later in his *Art poètique:* "Above all, let us have music. . . ."

But obviously he remains far behind the audacious Rimbaud. His caressing and gentle poetic temperament continues to play about within the frame of rhymes, his cajoling tenderness is lulled by veiled and hushed singing:

> *Car nous voulons la nuance encore,*
> *Pas la couleur, rien que la nuance.*

> For we still desired the nuance,
> Not color, nothing but nuance.

On the other hand, Rimbaud loves the shock of brilliant colors, a cascade of striking images, the flux and reflux of rhythmed prose.

There is, besides, a fundamental difference between the two poets. Both may be Bohemians and vagabonds, but Rimbaud is pre-eminently a person of mind and will; whereas Verlaine is sentimental and weak. The adolescent, despite his child-like face, like "a fallen angel," as some one has said, has a lucid and acute intelligence, a savage energy. The other man, with his mask at once of a Tartar and a faun, is the "poor Lélian," who cannot exist without loving and sinning.

Rimbaud is a visionary, a mad idealist. No compromise is possible in his intractable soul; he adjusts himself neither to literature nor to society; he will leave Europe and curse civilization. Verlaine will drag his poetry through public-houses and hospitals; he will wander through churches and brothels; he will pass artlessly from the lowest dives to the confessional. He is all weakness and compromise.

Shall I, at this point, become involved in the vexing, the endless debate in which so many have fruitlessly engaged? It is true—by no means surprising —that there was an ardent friendship between the two men, whose natures were so opposed and so complementary. In Verlaine's case, this friendship took on a passionate, exacting, jealous tone, a morbid character. Shall I say, with the enemies of Rimbaud and the partisans of Mme. Verlaine, that there was something else between them, what the judgment in the separation suit calls frankly, "an abominable relationship"? Biographers with as different tendencies as Lepelletier, Bourguignon and Houin, Delahaye and Berrichon, contemporaries and friends of the two poets, like Louis Pierquin, all seem to agree in answering *no*. M. Marcel Coulon ably champions the opposite thesis.

Shall I, in my turn, institute a trial, set up briefs, align proofs, interpret texts? Verlaine and Rimbaud, in verse and prose, have frequently made the most equivocal and also the most contradictory statements. On the one hand we have to deal with questionable confessions, on the other with sincere autobiography, but frightfully modified and deformed. What can one conclude? Against the evidence of disturbing pages like Verlaine's poem: *Laeti et er-*

107

rabundi, and especially the sonnet: *le Poète et la Muse,* written "in reference to a room in the rue Campagne-Première," one can always set up the formal denials of his letters to Lepelletier. Against the *Délires* of the *Saison en enfer,* we can oppose the no less definite deposition of Rimbaud after the Brussels incident. What is the truth? From all these texts, examined with any particular thesis in mind, one can derive whatever "truth" one is seeking.

Only one fact stands out from all the mass of conjecture: the accusation of the moralists agrees completely with everything that we know, from other sources, of the life of Verlaine, of his sensual instability, of his—shall we say—varied debauches, of his ungovernable and faun-like lechery. But it does not at all seem to be in harmony with what we know of Rimbaud, of his egotistic, cerebral, savagely closed nature. "Little passion," Verlaine himself wrote, "is discoverable in his rather intellectual and on the whole chaste odyssey." He never gives himself, either to God or to man.

Did Rimbaud lend himself to the sexual whims of Verlaine, to the obscenities of *Hombres,* surrounded as he was by the promiscuity and temptations of a rather sordid bohemianism, either through moral indifference, or through systematic irregularity and the curiosity of the "seer," or perhaps in sport, out of bravado or cynicism? It has not been proved, and to my mind it is hardly probable, but it is after all possible, and I insist that it has not the importance that most persons seem to attach to it. At this time

Rimbaud was just seventeen, and, in spite of his brief adventure of February, 1871, he was only a schoolboy. His sexual experiences were in no way more monstrous than those of any adolescent going through puberty. There really is nothing here to make any one cry out "perversion!" Rimbaud never became the slave of a habit, and it was certainly not he who led Verlaine astray. Let us then leave the discussion of these indiscretions and assume that Rimbaud's declarations before the court in Brussels were true. So much the worse for the disciples of Freud and readers avid of erotic theories and psychoanalysis!

But whatever the truth may be, certain it is that when Rimbaud left Paris in April, 1872, after remaining there for six months, Verlaine's friendship was powerless to retain him, or to assuage his irritation and his revolt against the type of literature then in vogue. He left with Verlaine the manuscript of the *Chasse spirituelle* which has not yet been recovered, and came back to Charleville to live there somewhat alone. The whole day long he would wander about the surrounding country as if in the grip of some dream, while night found him hard at work on the beginning of his *Illuminations*. "But all this leads to nothing practical," his mother would say. "So much the worse, but it must be done!" was his reply.

It had to be done—yes—even to the point of exhaustion, until he consumed himself, until he became mad with it. He was not the man to give in, to adjust

109

himself to petty artifices, to the literary fashions, to the conventions and traditions of coteries. He had returned from Paris more disgusted than ever. What! The art that was to redeem mankind, the art of the "seer," was to be the appanage of a few esthetes with monocles, of a few elegant parlor Parnassians? Ah, stupid civilization! Why hadn't the Communists burnt down the cupola of the Institute? More and more, as time goes on, Rimbaud ranged himself on the' opposing side of all existing things.

He works so hard to make himself a "seer" that he succeeds finally in making himself sick. He begins to wear himself out by "long, immense, logical irregularity of all the senses." And he arrives at what he will later call, "one of his follies," the alchemy of the word.

"I invented the color of the vowels! A black, E white, I red, O blue, U green. I determined the form and the movement of every consonant, and, by means of instinctive rhythms, I flattered myself that I had invented a poetic language that would one day or another be accessible to all the senses. I reserved the right of translation. . . . I wrote silences, nights, I noted the inexpressible. I fixated vertigoes."

A heroic conception of the function of the poet, in which he expresses his immense pride, his devouring and adventurous nature, but one that leads him, obviously, straight to the edge of the abyss. In reacting against coteries and the literary fashions of the day, he seeks originality in and against

110

everything, even despite his own natural inclinations. The acute realist, the implacable observer, fetters the visionary in him; in order to rid himself of them he has recourse to alcohol and hashish. Clear-minded naturally, he courts obscurity. His vigorous and hardy thought, which in a single bound had leaped over all the great problems of life and society, loiters now among subtle combinations of words, delighting in verbal instrumentation and hypnotizing itself with vocables.

"The old tricks of poetry played an important part in my alchemy of the word. I accustomed myself to plain hallucination: quite frankly I used to see a mosque in place of a factory, a school of drums made by angels, carriages on the roads of heaven, a salon at the bottom of a lake; monsters, mysteries; a ballad title raised up horrors before me. Then I explained my magical sophistries with the hallucination of words. I ended by finding the disorder of my mind sacred."

There are places in the *Illuminations* where he succeeds marvelously: *Fleurs, Antique, Aube.* But who, in Paris, in 1872, was capable of admiring such audacious discoveries? The Parnassian school reigned supreme. Symbolism was not yet born. No, really, there was no place for Rimbaud in the Temple of the Muses, and Verlaine was the only one who appreciated "his diamond-like prose." Most poets among the "Vilains Bonhommes," if they had been acquainted with these gorgeous sketches, would have made a mouthful of them. They would have

111

rallied to the esthetics proclaimed not without humor, by their friend Francois Coppée:

> *Rimbaud, fumiste réussi,*
> *—Dans un sonnet que je déplore—*
> *Veut que les lettres O E I*
> *Forment le drapeau tricolore.*
> *En vain le Décadent pérore,*
> *Il faut, sans mais, ni car, ni si,*
> *Un style clair comme l'aurore. . . .*
> *. . . Les vieux Parnassiens sont ainsi.*

> Rimbaud, the clever joker,
> —In a sonnet which I deplore—
> Arranges the letters O, E, I,
> To form the tricolored flag.
> In vain the Decadent perorates,
> He writes in a style without *ifs* or *buts,*
> As clear as the leaden-hued dawn. . . .
> . . . The old Parnassians are like that.

VI

THE TWO BOHEMIANS

WHILE Rimbaud, back in Charleville, was exerting himself during long nights of hallucination in the effort to express the inexpressible, Verlaine in Paris was becoming more and more embittered. His brutal nervous states, induced by absinthe, distracted his wife, and on the other hand, her prosiness and recriminations wearied him unbearably. The birth of a son did not reconcile the couple, and Verlaine felt that he could no longer expect either understanding or indulgence at the hands of his family. Sadly he compared his arid and empty life to the days of the winter before, which had seemed so rich, so uncommonly stimulating. He missed Rimbaud.

In May, 1872, he summoned Rimbaud again to Paris. At first the boy lived in the rue Monsieur-le-Prince, later at the Hotel de Cluny, on the rue Victor-Cousin, near the Sorbonne. Besides Verlaine, he went about chiefly with Forain, Ponchon and Richepin. They were frequently seen together on the terraces of cafés on the Boulevard St. Michel. Rimbaud used to become intoxicated on absinthe, to

113

heighten, as he believed, his poetic faculties. "Drunkenness derived from the juice of this plant is the most delicate and quivering of garments," he wrote to Delahaye in June in a drunken letter filled with the most monstrous and impudent scatology, and in which he takes a frightful pleasure in mutilating the language and in piling on the filthiest incongruities.

He led an exhausting and abnormal life. "Nowadays I carry on at night. From midnight until five in the morning. Last month, my room in the rue Monsieur-le-Prince gave on a garden of the Lycée St. Louis. Under my narrow window were enormous trees. At three o'clock in the morning the candlelight paled: all the birds cried out in the trees at once: it was the end of night. No more work. I was compelled to look at the trees and the sky, transported as I was by the indescribable hour, the first hour of morning. I saw the dormitories of the lycée completely muffled. And already I could hear the jerky, sonorous, delicious noise of the garbage trucks on the boulevards. I smoked my pipe, spitting on the shingled roof below, as my room was in the garret. At five o'clock I went downstairs to buy some bread; that is the time. The laborers are on their way to work everywhere. For me, it is the time to get drunk at the wine-shops. I returned to eat and went to bed at seven o'clock in the morning just as the sun was bringing out the wood-lice from under the shingles. The first morning in summer, and December evenings are what have always delighted me here."

114

An astonishing document this, and exceedingly characteristic, in which he takes equal delight in filth and in the ecstasy of morning. All of Rimbaud is here, and it was undoubtedly in the course of one of these late vigils that he composed that brilliant poem in prose, with its many-sided glitter, its flames so pure and so crystalline: "I embraced the summer dawn. Nothing stirred as yet on the brow of the palaces. The fountain was deathly still. The encampments of shadow clung to the wood road. I walked, waking warm live breaths as I went, while precious stones looked on, and wings arose without a sound . . . I laughed at the waterfall, disheveled among the firs: at the silvery summit I recognized the goddess . . ."

But soon he wearied of Paris. On the seventh of June, Verlaine, leaving his house to go to a neighboring pharmacist, saw Rimbaud coming to meet him, a letter in his hand. "I was just bringing this note to your house. Paris disgusts me. I am going away to Belgium."

"What! You are leaving us like that, without warning?"

"Well, then, come with me."

"But see here, old chap, that's impossible. My wife is sick! I am on my way to the druggist's now."

"No, stop harping on your wife all the time. Come, I tell you. Let's go."

115

"And so," Verlaine reports to his friend Emile Le Brun, "I went along with him, naturally."

They intended first to get to Belgium by way of Arras, where Verlaine had friends and relatives. "Curious city," he wrote in *Mes prisons*, "full of Spanish buildings of the good seventeenth century and a few monuments of architecture among which is the most beautiful Gothic town-hall in France, barracks and convent, bells and drums. No commerce and little industry. A few wealthy people hide behind the tall, white-shuttered windows of their little mansions surrounded by lovely gardens. The population, well-to-do or poor, is home-loving, but of good stock."

They left Paris in the evening, at about ten o'clock, from the Gare du Nord, and arrived in Arras at break of day. What were they to do, while waiting for friends to wake up and hospitable doors to open? A turn about the town took but a short time. Should they have breakfast at the station restaurant? "Rimbaud, despite his extremely precocious gravity which sometimes went so far as to make him unpleasant, a gravity often mingled with outbursts of strange, macabre fantasies, and I, still a boy in spite of my twenty-six years, both had our minds turned that day in the direction of lugubrious pleasantry. *Cabrionesques*, what did we take it into our heads to do but to try to 'astonish' the few simple travelers there consuming their hot drinks, their sandwiches and their galantines sprinkled with such expensive Algerian wine!

116

"Among the hayseeds present there was at the right, I still remember, on our bench, at no great distance from us, a rather old fellow, dressed in a commonplace fashion, his old straw hat set on a somewhat square head, shaven, simple and yet sly, sucking at a penny cigar, and swilling a two-cent glass of beer, coughing and clearing his throat. His air as he listened to our conversation was less stupid than malicious." A wink to Rimbaud. Well, what do you say? Agreed? And our two jokesters begin to play the part of murderers and escaped convicts, speaking of their thefts, of their last murder, with many frightful and vivid details. Their neighbor, horrified, slips outside furtively and comes back with the police.

The suspects are conducted to the City Hall before a justice of the peace. "Rimbaud, after having signaled to me," said Verlaine, "burst into tears" as he entered the magistrate's office, whence he emerged later, his part well played, "his eyes still moist." Verlaine on the contrary took another tone, looked at the man of law haughtily, named his references, showed his papers and passports, and, bragging of his Metz origin, added with a displeased air that he had not chosen patriotically for France in order to be arrested in so arbitrary a manner. In brief, "after a short stormy silence, the magistrate—a be-whiskered face, still young, curly brown hair and spectacles—rang the bell and summoned the police-men, who were told: 'You will conduct these individ-uals to the railroad station, and see that they get on

117

the first train leaving for Paris.' I objected, saying that we had not yet had our lunch. 'You will see that they have lunch, but they must leave immediately afterward, and don't let them out of your sight until the train moves off.' And so the pseudo-bandits went off to "get a snack in a good eating-place" designated by the officer, and after offering a drop to the "nice cops," took the next train back to Paris.

They were not daunted by their experience. That same evening they passed directly from the Gare du Nord to the Gare de l'Est. Since they had been unable to reach Belgium through Arras, they determined to reach it through the Ardennes.

At Charleville they found the faithful Bretagne. The day fled by in carousing and other "jocosities," and toward midnight Bretagne stationed himself with them under the windows of a livery-stable keeper, known as Father Jean, whom he addressed in these terms: "Jean, brother, I have here with me two priests, friends of mine who have need of your offices. Get up and harness the beast of the Apocalypse!" During the preparations, Bretagne ran to his room, and brought back a guitar, an old silver watch and a two-franc piece, which he presented to the travelers. The two of them got up into the carriole and arrived at three o'clock in the morning at the first Belgian village, about fifteen kilometers from Charleville. In this way they avoided the railroad stations of the Meuse valley, Vireux or Givet, with their prying police and customs officers.

Having crossed the frontier, they continued on

foot toward Brussels, through Walcourt and Charleroi, across the "Belgian countryside," sung in the *Romances sans Paroles*.

> *Ginguettes claires,*
> *Bières, clameurs,*
> *Servantes chères*
> *A tous fumeurs!*
>
> *Gares prochaines,*
> *Gais chemins grands,*
> *Quelles aubaines!*
> *Bons juifs errants.* . . .

Jolly arbors,
Beer and noise
And sweet barmaids
For all good smokers!

The frequent halts
On the gay highways,
What great windfalls!
For good wandering Jews. . . .

During all this time Mme. Verlaine was consumed with anxiety and impatience. In spite of all the miseries of her married life, she could not willingly resign herself to being abandoned. She finally got on the track of the fugitives, and left with her mother for Belgium, where she rejoined her husband on July 21st. One can picture the scene, from the only passage that we have up to the present of Verlaine's unpublished memoirs. Return, she begs of him. Everything will be forgiven. But he must return! She is ready to expatriate herself, if she must, to be with him. Perhaps they need a change of air and mode of living. In the name of their child, let him return to her!

Verlaine seemed moved. For the moment he agreed and took the train back to France with the two women. At Quiévrain, the station on the frontier, everybody got off. "After the customs examination," his wife tells, "Verlaine disappeared and we could not find him. The train was about to leave and we had to decide to go without him. At the very moment that the gates were being closed we saw him finally on the platform. 'Get up, quickly,' my mother cried to him. 'No, I am staying!' he answered, shoving his hat down on his head with his fist.—I never saw him again."

The *Bonne Chanson* (Verlaine's poems celebrating his love affair with his wife), was silenced, then, muffled by the despotic chant of the *Bateau ivre*. To sea! To sea! Adventure! Yes, even though it lead to shipwreck, if only it be with Rimbaud. After a month of loafing and debauchery in Brussels, where they met the Communist Georges Cavalier, called Pipe-en-Bois, and a few other political exiles, the two friends left for England on September the 8th.

"In 1872," wrote Verlaine, "I set out for Dover from Ostend, one Saturday evening, with Arthur Rimbaud, the child poet. After a somewhat shaky crossing, the first that he or I had ever made, during the seven or eight hours of which we showed our sea-legs admirably, in spite of the example of seasickness given by most of our fellow-voyagers, we debarked during the night and slept over at Dover. The next day, the sun shining splendidly, we made a tour of the whole town, which is of moderate interest except for the admirable white cliffs which have given their name to England (Albion)."

They arrived in London the 10th of September. Rimbaud, as usual, had not a penny, and Verlaine paid for both. At first they felt themselves out of their element. They could hardly make themselves understood, they knew so little English. And then the very atmosphere seemed inhospitable to them. Ah! it was not the air of Paris, smart, light, stimulating. Where were the boulevard cafés, the welcoming terraces, the cordial waiters, full of humbug, yet so clever at spilling the ice-water, drop by drop, on the milky absinthe? "London is as flat as a melancholy bedbug. Little blackened houses or great Gothic or Venetian stone-boxes, four or five potable cafés, etc." There are only narrow, tiny bars, where one must "drink one's order" standing up. "You enter," said Verlaine, "through a terribly thick door, kept ajar by a tremendous strap, which (the door) strikes your buttocks after having in most instances grazed your hat. The interior of the bar is very small: at a mahogany counter, covered with zinc, along the length of which—either standing, or perched on very high and very narrow stools—you can see well-dressed gentlemen, poor derelicts, porters all in white, coachmen all puffed up like our coachmen and bristling like them, all of them drinking, smoking, and talking through their noses. Behind the counter are the barkeeps with their shirtsleeves rolled up, or young women, generally pretty, all with their hair disheveled, elegantly dressed but in poor taste, whom the men pummel with their hands, their canes, or their umbrellas, laughing out loud all the while, and apparently using coarse language which is far from offensive to them."

What decided inferiority in the Anglo-Saxons! In these bars, there is no talk. No half-serious, half frivolous conversation such as Verlaine used to love so much in the Parisian cafés. Rimbaud, solid and taciturn drinker, does not suffer from this.

> *Entre autres blâmables excès,*
> *Je crois que nous bûmes de tout. . . .*

> Among other faulty excesses,
> I think we drank of everything. . . .

Ah! if they had only drunk beer! But beside pale ale and the yeasty black stout, they had gin and golden whiskey and soda. Rimbaud, whose imagination was enormously stimulated by alcohol, dragged his friend from public-house to public-house around the shipping quarters of the Thames and London Bridge.

The docks! What a heady discovery! Ships of all nations, swarming longshoremen and sailors, their faces tanned, baked under their blue caps, pyramids of bales, packing boxes and cheap merchandise, odor of tar and fish, foreign tongues, and mysterious inscriptions! The chant of the *Bateau ivre* resounds secretly at the bottom of his dreams and calls him toward the sea. Rimbaud questions a shipmaster standing on a quay among the puddles of oily water, overseeing the loading of his vessel. He slips in among the ruddy-faced sailors in their colored jerseys, tries to see, to conjecture, to understand . . . but alas, his hour has not yet struck. He is not yet ready to get under sail. First he must learn English—indispensable language for his contemplated voyages. And the two idlers go slowly up toward the populous quarters of Houndsditch and Whitechapel.

Here are the "cells of public houses, so much like the inside of a pomegranate," with their varnished, polished woodwork, with the golden patina "as in a Delacroix background," with their panes of beveled glass, their shining copper pots and the gleam of the whiskey in the glasses. Here are to be found the leprous façades, the little black bricks and the green sash-windows, where hang placards in Hebrew and whence Rembrandtesque Jews come forth. And everywhere the poor, "with their pale coloring, their drawn features, their long skeleton-like hands, their sparse beards, their sad blondish hair."

In Verlaine's *Croquis Londoniens*, which in default of other documents permit us to reconstruct the life of Rimbaud in London, we can perceive everywhere the influence that he exercised over Verlaine. Here one finds an echo of his impiety—his scorn for "open air sermons and extortion by hymn-singing . . . church-doings and other mummeries . . ." There is also a strangely powerful and realistic note on the City, its banks and its warehouses. "The docks suffice for my more and more modernistic poetics." This is a far cry from the *Fêtes Galantes* and their stylized ornamentations, far from blue gardens in the moonlight, far from "tall svelte fountains among the marbles." The city, "black as a crow and as clamorous as ducks, prudish in the manner of all vice, and tipsy everlastingly," extends its ocean of bricks and smoke farther than the eye can reach. The two vagabonds push as far as Woolwich in the course of a long walk which Verlaine describes in a tone of astonishment: "The docks are unbelievable, Carthage, Tyre and all united, no?" Is this not a vision from *Villes*, in the *Illuminations?*

But the two poets do not frequent only the bars and the docks. Their resources are almost exhausted and they try to earn some money. They attach themselves to a few Frenchmen, revolutionists and idealists like themselves, former communists driven out of France by the victory of the *Versaillais*. In these warm and quarrelsome meetings at the café de la Sablonière et de Provence, in Leicester Square, Rimbaud rediscovers with pleasure an atmosphere of revolt and fantasy, the odor of battle. There he finds Eugène Vermesch of Lille, condemned to death after the Commune for the publication of *Père Duchesne*, journalists like Lissagaray and Jules Andrieu, friend of the young Madox Brown, and in particular the painter Felix Regamey, who used to attend the dinners of the "Vilains Bonhommes" and who now lived in a studio in Langham Street.

"Verlaine," wrote Regamey, "is handsome in his way, and although very ill provided with linen, hardly looks like a man who is crushed by his bad luck. But he is not alone. A silent comrade accompanies him, one likewise not distinguished for his elegance. It is Rimbaud." The kind-hearted artist has also left a few sketches in which he reveals in turn the financial grandeur and decadence of the two poets. In one, Rimbaud, sunk into a chair, a linen bag in his hand, disappears under a high hat which cost him ten shillings and which he will carry back to Charleville with pride. In the other, the two vagabonds slink along under the distrustful eye of a policeman, pipe in hand, hungry, with a gallows look, their clothes torn, their top-pieces in dreadful condition, beard and hair in disorder. . . .

Let us follow them. "Every day we take long walks in the suburbs and the surrounding country, Kew, Woolwich, etc., till all London is known to us. Drury Lane, Whitechapel, Pimlico, Angel, the City, Hyde Park conceal no mystery from us." They go into filthy low cafés or "dives for traveling salesmen" in Leicester Square. From these they go to that friendly "public-house," 6 Old Compton Street, where Vermesch gave a lecture on Blanqui in November and read one of Verlaine's poems on the glory of violence. ("*O cloître Saint-Merry* . . .") Then they go up toward the north and come back

125

again in the evening to Vermesch's former lodging, a furnished room that he had occupied before his marriage, 35 Howland Street, in the rear of a great house in the Adam style, with high, ornamented windows. It was there—behind that façade marked today with a commemorative plaque dedicated by His Excellency the Comte de Saint Aulaire, French ambassador to England—that our two communists completed, one the *Romances sans paroles*, and the other the *Illuminations*.

For life was not all dreaming, drinking and smoking. They were working too. "We are studying English hard, Rimbaud and I, from the works of Edgar Poe, from the collections of popular songs, from Robertson, etc. Our faulty pronunciation makes us tell fibs to the tradespeople, at the public-houses and book-shops." Verlaine also does some "American work that pays rather well," and gives lessons. Rimbaud also suddenly styles himself a teacher, finds modest employment in some business, and risks himself as far as the Rotunda of the British Museum. "Here I am steeped in poetry, in intelligent companionship, in purely literary and serious conversation," writes Verlaine on the 8th of November. "We have a very small circle of artists and literary men. And now they come to throw me out of my quasi-hermitage and make me write memoranda and letters to magistrates."

It was true; his wife was entering a suit for separation, naming the "abominable relationship" between Verlaine and Rimbaud as cause. But he does

126

not suffer himself to be drawn in, struggles, directs his defense, looks for witnesses. "Rimbaud," he confides to his friend Lepelletier, on November 14th, "has written to his mother recently to inform her of everything that is being said against us, and I am at present in regular correspondence with her." Yes—and this is not the least amusing aspect of the story—the close-fisted woman actually sets herself to work, is "very much interested in the matter." Let no one impugn the honor of her offspring! She may reprimand him herself, but she permits no one else to suspect his morals.

But Rimbaud has another plan in mind in interesting his mother. He wants to regain his liberty and also the manuscripts that he had left in Paris in the rue Nicolet. Fearing legal complications, he despatches his mother to Verlaine's parents-in-law. He gives her to understand that he can easily have those despised poems accepted by a publisher. Their publication would be a kind of business reference for him, and might aid him to get a job, to earn money. On this Madame Rimbaud leaves for Paris. But in vain. The manuscript of the *Chasse spirituelle* has never been found.

The 26th of December Verlaine wrote to Lepelletier: "Very sad. All alone. Rimbaud (whom you do not know, who is known only to me) is no longer here. Frightful void." The little room in Howland Street, near Tottenham Court Road, is terribly gloomy in this sad winter weather, these days steeped in yellow fog and streaked with dirty gray rain.

127

Il pleure dans mon coeur
Comme il pleut sur la ville. . . .

There is weeping in my heart,
Like the rain o'er the town. . . .

☆ VII ☆

THE BRUSSELS DRAMA

A ll alone." Abandoned then? Yes, Verlaine had been left to drag himself about, alone and bored, in the sad London streets. His fantastic friend, accustomed to making freakish and impulsive decisions, had suddenly deserted him. He had wearied of Verlaine's indecision, complaints, remorse. The interminable stories of the separation suit irritated him beyond measure. Everything tended to divide them more and more.

Verlaine could not altogether succeed in shaking off his old love, the love for his wife. The *Bonne Chanson* of other days echoed in the depths of his memory, and in his moments of spleen he would yield himself to vain regrets. The past still had a grip on him.

The other man, on the contrary, bent himself feverishly upon the future, felt himself changing, becoming "a new man." The poet in him was dying. Almost all the *Illuminations* had been written. The thirst for knowledge, power, conquest—a sharp desire for positive possession this time—tortured him. He was concerned no longer with the problem of

"reinventing love" (if that ever was a problem) nor
of inventing "new flowers, new perfumes, etc.," of
devising a new language and new rhythms. What
he wanted now was to know English. This was
enough, and it was everything. But in order to at-
tain this knowledge he had to work at it constantly,
abandon poetic reveries, political and social utopias,
study grammars and dictionaries, abandon Bohemia.

This meant also that he must abandon Verlaine,
and Rimbaud did not hesitate. Hardly had he re-
turned to the Ardennes, however, at the end of
December, 1872, than "poor Lélian" fell sick in
London, and, to tell the truth, so seriously, that his
days were thought to be numbered. His mother, ac-
companied by one of his cousins, flew to his bedside.
But all this feminine solicitude was not enough for
him: he called for his friend.

Rimbaud did not fail him: with fifty francs sent
him by the sick man's mother he set out on his
way. At the end of January, 1873, Verlaine wrote
to Lepelletier: "Two days after, Rimbaud, who had
been gone from here for a month, returned, and
his care, joined with that of my mother and my
cousin, has succeeded in saving me this time . . .
from a crisis that would have been mortal had I
been alone." But now in his turn, the adolescent
began to weaken. His health had been shattered, and
these first months of the year 1873 were marked
by serious disorders: fever, languor, visions, hallu-
cinations, and above all by a morbid irritability.
He continued to grow, and at the same time became

130

thinner before one's very eyes. Bitter price for his latest excesses, alcohol, hashish, tobacco above all! Consequently, at the end of a few days, when he saw that Verlaine was on the road to recovery, he returned to the Ardennes and rejoined his family at Roche, in the neighborhood of Vouziers, on the property that had been left to Mme. Rimbaud by her father.

This old house was not a very comfortable residence. It had been ravaged in 1870 by the Germans, and in 1873, Paterne Berrichon tells us, the ruins of the stables were still covered over with wild hop vine and nettles. Everybody had to lend a hand in the work of rebuilding. Rimbaud assisted the workmen with pick and shovel when needed. But he still had something to say and so he began his *Saison en enfer*, "a kind of prodigious psychological autobiography," said Verlaine, "written in that diamond-like prose which is his exclusive gift."

Picture him then: thin, his face gray, without vigor and without joy, in that house devastated like his own youth. The flat countryside has not the freshness and variety of the country about Charleville, and it does not attract him. He crouches there in the courtyard for hours, his manuscript on his knees. "I am seated among broken pots and nettles, leprous at the bottom of a wall corroded by the sun." He sees again his "mendicant" childhood, does not regret "his old share in divine gayety," but "the sober air of this crabbed countryside feeds his atrocious pessimism actively."

131

At about the same time that he settles himself at Roche, Verlaine, convalescent, comes "to pasture" in the Belgian Ardennes, at Jehonville. This is a period of calm and happy repose for him. The walks round about this picturesque country of Bouillon, the rustic and wholesome fare, the healthful air of the forest, the sinuous caress of the Semoy and the song of its clear waters, its rapids full of fish, all this does him good. He has finished his *Romances sans paroles*, in which are included both "Belgian Landscapes" and "London Sketches." He is full of pleasant memories of his friend, to whom he wishes to dedicate his book. Calmer now, he summons Rimbaud to meet him. Are they not both cured? Why not see each other again? Who knows, perhaps take up the good free amusing life of adventure again, return together to England?

The first meeting-place he suggests is Bouillon, on the 18th of May. But Rimbaud will not budge. He had begun writing, in April, those "little stories in prose" that he planned for a while to call "pagan book" or "negro book," and which were destined later to find a place in a *Saison en enfer*. He works over it feverishly and with passion. He will brook no delay, no interruption. He must finish this work that obsesses him, from which his mother naïvely expects the promised bookshop success, and into which he pours—for himself alone—all his bitterness.

"My *mother*," he writes in May to Ernest Delahaye, "has put me into this sad hole. I don't know how I'll get out of it, but I shall manage it somehow.

I long for that atrocious *Charlestown* (Charleville), the Universe café, the Library, etc. I am working, however, rather steadily. I am writing little stories in prose, general title: pagan book or negro book. It is silly and innocent. Oh innocence, innocence, innoc . . . a plague on it! . . . I am abominably irritated. Not a single book here. Not a single public-house within reach, not a single incident in the street. What a horror this French countryside is! My fate depends on this book, for which I have yet to devise half a dozen atrocious stories. How can one invent atrocities here?" He adds in closing: "Shortly I shall send you stamps to buy and send me Goethe's *Faust* in a popular edition. It ought to cost a penny for the post."

Delahaye was then at Charleville, and Verlaine had summoned him also to Bouillon. After some vacillation, a meeting of the three friends was decided on for the 24th of May. The dinner, enlivened by smutty stories, was very gay. The springtime sang in the new-washed sky, the old château of Godfroy was dressed in young green leaves and the silvery waters of the Semoy (whose succulent trout they had just eaten) flowed through the groves in a swift laughing current, inviting vagabondage. To your health, O Springtime! The glasses clink and bottles are emptied! And the next day, May 25th, the two poets embark once again for England, this time from Antwerp.

The experiment was disastrous this time, as might have been expected. Rimbaud was excessively ner-

133

vous. He regretted having followed the "poor brother," could not forgive himself, considered himself humiliated. Hardly had he arrived in London than he gave Verlaine the slip, leaving him alone for days at a time, irritating him in the evening with bickerings. It was probably at this time that Rimbaud met "that rare, if not unique London woman," of whom Verlaine speaks. It was in the arms of this expert mistress that he first learned the arts of love in facile embrace and voluptuous surfeit. "In the morning—dawn of a discordant June day—I ran to the fields like an ass, blaring and flourishing my wrongs, until the Sabine women of the suburbs came to throw themselves on my breast."

He had detached himself completely from Verlaine. Exasperated by his drunken complaints, by his "idiotic grief," he used to take his revenge at night. He would wake him with a start, take malicious pleasure in frightening him, defied him and made fun of him in turn. Ah, what "frightful vigils" he spent near that "satanic doctor"! When the disputes were finished, he permitted Verlaine to fall asleep, grumbling, on his pallet, and, opening the window, breathed in the cool night air, indifferent to his friend's misery. "I would create," he wrote in *Vagabonds*, "phantoms of future nocturnal luxury beyond the countryside, interspersed with bands of rare music. After this vaguely hygienic distraction, I would stretch myself out on my cot. And, almost every night, as soon as I had fallen asleep, the poor brother would get up, his mouth stinking, his eyes

starting from his head—just as he dreamed himself!
—and drag me into the other room howling his
dream of idiotic grief. I had really, in all sincerity,
taken it on myself to restore him to his original state
as child of the Sun—and so we wandered, nourished
by the wine of the cellars and the traveler's biscuit.
I in a hurry to find the place and the formula."

Things went from bad to worse until, at the end
of July, a quarrel as violent as it was stupid broke
out. They were living in London behind King's
Cross, in Camden Town, Great College Street, and
did their own housekeeping and cooking. On that
day it was Verlaine's turn to go to market for pro-
visions. He was on his way home, then, carrying a
herring and a liter of oil. Rimbaud spied on him
from the window, sneering and mocking at his ap-
pearance noisily. "God, how awkward you look! How
dumb with your bottle and your dirty fish. If you
could only see yourself, you old man!" The "old
man" climbed up the stairs, grumbling and swear-
ing, opened the door, and was met by a broadside
of insults and sarcasm. Then, drunk with rage and
whiskey, he threw the herring in Rimbaud's face,
tumbled down the stairs again and disappeared in
the street. He also—at the end—had had enough
of this tyrannical, sharp-tongued boy. Since he will
not change, Verlaine leaves him flat—without a
penny. Let him shift for himself and endure hard-
ship. That will train him! After this conventional
"desertion," Verlaine takes the boat back to Bel-
gium.

135

He has decided to get back into his wife's good graces, and deludes himself that she will consent to a reconciliation. Through the mediation of his mother, he proposes a meeting with her at Brussels. But it is, alas, too late; nothing can persuade his wife to agree to a reconciliation that she believes will be at best a temporary one, and the elder Mme. Verlaine arrives alone in Brussels to meet him. Verlaine is furious at his wife, and overcome with remorse at having left his friend without resources on the streets of London. He begs Rimbaud to return and sends him money for his crossing.

Rimbaud got off the boat at Brussels on July 8th, and installed himself at the Hotel Liègois, rue Pachéco, not far from the Botanical Gardens. It was here that the drama took place.

It has often been told, and I have no intention of retelling it in my own way. The story as told by Rimbaud in his deposition before the judges follows:

"I made the acquaintance of Verlaine in Paris two years ago. Last year, after certain disagreements with his wife and her family, Verlaine proposed to me that I go abroad with him. We were to earn our living in one way or another, for I have no personal fortune and Verlaine has only what he makes from his writing and a little money given him by his mother. We came to Brussels together in July of last year and remained here about two months. Seeing that there was nothing for us to do in this city we went on to London. We lived there together until very recently, occupying the same lodgings

136

and pooling our resources. As a result of a discussion that we had at the beginning of last week, caused by my reproaching him for his indolence and his way of acting toward certain of our acquaintances,[1] Verlaine left me without warning and without even telling me where he was going. I supposed, however, that he was going to Brussels or that he would pass through here, because he had taken the boat to Antwerp. I later received a letter from him written on board ship, which I will give you, announcing his intention of returning to his wife. He added that if she rejected his proposal he would kill himself within three days. He gave his mailing address as Poste Restante, Brussels. I afterwards wrote him two letters in which I asked him to come back to London or to consent to my coming to meet him in Brussels; that I wanted to join him again as we had had no reason to separate.[2]

"I left London then, arriving in Brussels Tuesday morning, and met Verlaine. His mother was with him. His plans were indefinite. He did not care to remain in Brussels, fearing that he could find no employment in this city. I for my part did not want to return to London as he proposed, for our departure must have produced a very disagreeable impression on our friends, and besides, I had resolved to go back to Paris. At times Verlaine showed a

[1] Rimbaud's version here differs slightly from the account that Verlaine gave to his friend Emile Le Brun and from Ernest Delahaye's explanation (the story of the fish as recounted above).

[2] This does not give the correct impression. Rimbaud's eagerness to find Verlaine again can be explained only by financial reasons: he did not have a cent and wanted to return to France.

137

disposition to accompany me, to go, as he expressed it, to do justice to his wife and his parents-in-law. At times he refused to accompany me because Paris recalled memories that were too depressing. He was very wrought up. However, he insisted continually that I stay with him, sometimes desperately, sometimes furiously. There was no sequence in his ideas. Wednesday evening he became very drunk. Thursday morning he went out at six o'clock, returning at noon, drunk again. He showed me a pistol that he had bought, and when I asked him what he intended doing with it, he answered jokingly, 'It's for you, for me, for everybody!' He was excessively excited.

"While we were together in our room, he went downstairs several times again to get something to drink. He argued continually against my returning to Paris. I had made up my mind, however. I even asked his mother for the price of a ticket. At a certain moment he locked the door of the room opening on the hall and sat down on a chair with his back against the door. I was standing leaning against the opposite wall. Then he said: 'Here's what you get, since you will go!' or something like that. He pointed his pistol at me and fired a shot which struck me in the left wrist. The first shot was almost immediately followed by a second, but this time the weapon was not directed at me but lowered toward the floor.

"Verlaine instantly expressed the most intense regret for what he had done. He hurled himself into
138

the next room, the one occupied by his mother, and threw himself on the bed; he was like a madman. He put his pistol into my hands and implored me to fire at him. His attitude was one of profound sorrow for what had happened. Toward five o'clock in the evening, his mother and he brought me here [3] to have the wound dressed. When we returned to the hotel, Verlaine and his mother proposed that I remain with them so that they could take care of me, or that I return to the hospital until I was completely cured. As the wound seemed to me very slight, I expressed the intention of returning to France that very evening, to my mother in Charleville. This precipitated a new outburst of despair on the part of Verlaine. His mother gave me twenty francs for the railroad fare and they both set out to accompany me to the Gare du Midi.

"Verlaine was like a madman; he tried every expedient to keep me from going. Besides, he had his hand constantly in his coat pocket where he kept his pistol. When we arrived at the Place Rouppe he got a few steps ahead of us and then came back toward me. His attitude was so alarming that I feared a new outburst of madness. I turned around and took to my heels. It was then that I asked a policeman to arrest him. The bullet in my hand has not yet been extracted. The doctor in charge here has told me that this can only be done after two or three days."

The judicial investigation from then on took the

[3] At the infirmary of the Saint-Jean Hospital, in Brussels.

form of questions and answers, and although the rest has no connection with the drama, properly speaking, I quote it here for its psychological and documentary interest.

Q. What was your source of income in London?

A. Principally the money that Mme. Verlaine sent to her son. We also gave French lessons together, but these lessons did not bring in much, about twelve francs a week, toward the end.

Q. Do you know the reason for the disagreement between Verlaine and his wife?

A. Verlaine did not want his wife to continue to live in her father's house.

Q. Does she not also complain about your intimacy with Verlaine?

A. Yes, she even accuses us of immoral relations. But I shan't even bother to deny such calumny.

Such is Rimbaud's deposition, duly reread and signed by him July 12th, 1873. It does not agree completely in all details with other accounts. The scene has been described several times and with variations by Verlaine himself. Edmond Lepelletier has evoked it very vividly, after the memories of the poet's mother, who tends naturally to excuse her son. For Berrichon, on the contrary, Rimbaud was the angelic victim of a madman. After reading these different accounts it is obvious that Verlaine was more deeply in the wrong, and that he prejudiced his case still further by his alcoholic excesses and his criminal attack. However, one cannot avoid the conclusion that Rimbaud sought to rid himself of Verlaine by having him arrested.

Verlaine was condemned to two years in jail and was sent to the prison of Mons. Rimbaud went back to the Ardennes, his arm in a sling. It was the end of their double Bohemia. *Laeti et errabundi*, they had seen everything, tried everything, exhausted everything:

> *Fleuves et monts, bronzes et marbres,*
> *Les couchants d'or, l'aube magique,*
> *L'Angleterre, mère des arbres,*
> *Fille des beffrois, la Belgique.*

> Rivers and mountains, marble and bronze,
> Golden sunsets, magic dawns,
> England, mother of trees,
> Belgium, daughter of belfries.

☆ VIII ☆

THE DEATH OF CHIMERAS

JULY 20th, 1873. Rimbaud, not finding his mother in Charleville, was forced to return to the farm at Roche. Claudel has described this region of Vouziers very delicately, "poor harvests, a small group of slate roofs, and always on the horizon the illusory line of forests. Country of springs where the limpid water, imprisoned in its own depth, turns upon itself; the glaucous Aisne, laden with water-lilies and with three long reeds emerging from the jade green water." From the station at Vonq to Roche is a distance of several kilometers. Rimbaud, wounded, made them on foot.

I can see him, his bandaged hand borne in a sling, taking long strides along the dusty road. It is noon. Around him stretch the fields of silvery oats. He approaches the house.

At this time Roche was a hamlet of about a dozen families. A great house, somewhat damaged by the Revolution, still retained the pompous and excessive title of "château." However, this was not where the Rimbaud family lived. Their house was on the main road between Vouziers and Attigny. A wagon-
142

house, giving access to the courtyard of the farm and surmounted by a dovecote, flanked it on one side and gave it an important, sturdy appearance. Claudel recalls the façade of corroded stone with its high peasant roofing, and the date 1791 over the doorway. The windows were protected by iron bars. The door, studded with nails, opened on a central corridor from which the stairway rose. On the right was the kitchen, on the left, the dining-room.

Rimbaud enters. They had been told of his coming, he is expected. His arm? "Oh, it's nothing. A scratch! I've something else to think about!" He falls into a chair in the kitchen, his head in his hands, and bursts into sobs. "Verlaine! Verlaine!" They can drag nothing else out of him. The crisis passes. They sit down to eat. His mother asks him: "And your papers. Have they been returned to you?" "No, they are lost. Besides, I don't care, I don't want to see them any more." Then he relapses into silence.

The next day he locks himself up carefully in the bare and whitewashed granary on the floor which has been assigned to him as sleeping quarters. He paces up and down this garret and will see no one. He is witnessing his own defeat, and contemplating the fall of his own mephistophelian undertaking. "Once on a time, if I remember rightly, my life was a feast where all hearts were opened, where all wines flowed. One evening I took Beauty upon my knee and found her bitter. I abused her. O sorceresses, O misery, O hate, it is to you my treasure has been entrusted."

143

He has indeed made the stealthy bound of the wild beast on joy. "I have stretched myself out in the mud. I have dried myself in the air of crime." Enraged at himself, he continues his tirade. He strikes at his last remaining idols dumbly.

When his mother ventures by chance up the wooden staircase, she hears muffled sobs, jeers, cries of anger, frightful blasphemies. He has succeeded in writing his book of the damned; he is scribbling the last sheets of *Une saison en enfer.*

The little book, when finished, was given to a printers' union to be set up, the Alliance Typographique, 37, rue aux Choux, in Brussels, and was to be sold at one franc the copy. But no sooner was it printed than Rimbaud, struck by some new whim, lost interest and refused to pay for the printing. The edition remained concealed in the dust of the print-shop until 1901, when a Belgian bibliophile, M. Losseau, discovered it by chance. As far as the poet was concerned it ceased to exist. Perhaps he might even have destroyed a few author's copies, which would be the basis for the legend that he collected all his works and burnt them in the fire-place at Roche in one grand auto-da-fé.

Une saison en enfer! How many commentaries have appeared on this mysterious autobiography! Some have seen in it, as in a burst of light, Rimbaud's conversion to Christianity; others have discovered in it his immutable atheism. The truth is that both states are present, but in conflict. The hell he speaks of is at bottom that inexplicable battle

144

between the forces of good and of evil, struggling for, tearing out the soul of the poet. Angel or devil, elect or damned? He is both. He is a man, but a man heroically, insatiably greedy, gifted with superhuman powers of revolt and self-denial, desperately athirst for the good, and yet experiencing in evil an intoxicating and savage voluptuousness.

There is within him a pagan and a Christian, but the Christian does not gain the mastery. Hell is the rebellion of the pagan, of the barbarian, of the "negro," as he says, of the "child of the sun," against the morality, tradition, the gentle slavery of Christianity. Atrocious and harrowing torment! If Christ had not come, there would have been no sin. Man would have always known the joy of living. Primitive nature would have flowered, far from artificial ethics, far from lying constrictions and discipline. Two voices arise, one that he has already heard in his mythological poem: *Soleil et chair,* the voice of Venus, "Divine mother, marine Aphrodite"; and the other, the voice of Jesus who, on his bitter road, "yokes us to his cross." Cursed baptism! This is what has created the schism in his unruly soul. Two men in him answer: *Credo in unam . . . Credo in unum Deum.* He is exposed to the assault of hostile forces.

The true, the primitive man in him is he who vaunts his *Mauvais sang.* "I have inherited from my Gallic ancestors the blue-white eye, a narrow brain, and awkwardness in combat. From them I have also inherited idolatry and the love of sacrilege; oh! all

145

vices, anger, lust—lust is magnificent—above all lying and laziness." The real Rimbaud is he who exclaims: "Priests, professors, schoolmasters, you are wrong to turn me over to justice, I have never been one of those people; I have never been a Christian; I am one of the race that sang under torture; I do not understand laws; I have no moral sense, I am a brute." He is, he says himself, "a wild beast, a negro."

But another voice cries out in him: "The whites are landing. Cannon! We must submit to baptism, dress ourselves, work. I have received the stroke of grace in my heart." And then, hurried, avid, exalted, this other voice seeks to dominate the song of his ancestors. "Divine love alone grants the keys of knowledge. I see that nature is a spectacle of goodness. Good-by chimeras, ideals, errors! The logical song of the angels arises from the ship of salvation: it is divine love. . . . Reason is born in me. The world is good. I shall bless life. I shall love my brother. These are no longer the promises made to children nor the hope of escaping old age or death. God is my strength and I praise God."

However, the damned one sneers in return: "I do not believe that I am embarked upon a wedding tour with Jesus Christ for a father-in-law . . . I have said God. I want *liberty* in salvation." From then on is developed the terrible conflict between eternal affirmation and eternal negation, as in the famous passage from Carlyle. But the internal duel of *Sartor Resartus* has neither the despairing fierceness

146

nor the grandeur of hallucination of the *Nuit de l'Enfer*. All phases of the battle between demons and archangels succeed each other here, clashing, violent, portrayed with livid clarity. It is a night of vertigo and tempest, full of blasphemy and prayers, traversed by strident cries, peopled with phantoms, ecstasies and nightmares. "I had caught a glimpse of my conversion to virtue and happiness, my salvation. Will I be able to describe the vision? The air of hell suffers no hymns! There were millions of charming creatures, a sweet spiritual concert, strength and peace, noble ambitions, what else?" Everything vanishes, and the damned soul, recovering himself, hurls his challenge. "I am the slave of my baptism. Parents, you contrived my misfortune and your own." Ah, if he could only find again his primitive strength, his whole victorious paganism. "Hell cannot touch the heathen." But no, the original state is lost forever. Christianity has wrapped life in darkness by the menace of sin, and has lit the infernal fires. It is too late. The soul is the prey of good and bad demons. Listen to these panting voices, these furious responses, these despairing lamentations: "Enough! . . . of those errors they deplore in me—magic, false perfumes, puerile music. And say that I hold the truth, that I see justice: I have a sound and steady judgment, I am ready for perfection . . . Pride—my scalp is parched. Pity, O Lord, I am afraid. I am thirsty, so thirsty. Ah, childhood, the grass, the rain, the pool on the rocks, the moonlight when the belfry clock strikes twelve . . .

147

The devil is in the belfry at that hour. Mary! Holy
Virgin! What stupid horror!" And the crisis con-
tinues, implacable, a veritable access of madness
which seeks its paroxysm in an exasperated appeal
for suffering: "I demand! I demand! a fork thrust,
—a drop of fire!"

But in reality, how can he be saved? In *Une saison
en enfer* there is no longer a possibility of Redemp-
tion. Let us examine closely the first chapter of *Dé-
lires*. What irony! What disdain! And what pride
in evil! The damned soul has only sarcasm for the
weak, for those who submit. The accents of a Byron
are nothing beside his. One might almost say that
Rimbaud has a presentiment of Verlaine's conver-
sion: "the infernal bridegroom" has only contempt
for the "foolish virgin." He parodies "the confession
of a companion in Hell" and mimics the unhappy re-
pentant: "Pardon, divine master, pardon! Ah! par-
don! How many tears! And how many tears still to
come, I hope!" He would not humiliate himself so.
For himself, he makes "glory out of infamy," "a
delight out of cruelty," he is "of a distant race,"
and it is impossible "to enter into his world." Al-
ways the same obsession, the obsession of primitive
nature, at once pure and impure, virginal and ra-
diantly blooming. Heaven was not then covered
with clouds, it was resplendent with glorious pagan
light. No baptism was needed. Man was god. All
our suffering is derived from that. The negro and
the Oriental wanted to live in the Christian tradition,
according to the laws of Western civilization. The
148

spirit of the poet "wants absolutely to take upon itself all the cruel developments the spirit has undergone since the end of Oriental civilization," but it is not adapted to the Western code. "Crowns of martyrdom, triumphs of art, pride of inventors, ardor of pirates—I bade them all go to the devil. I turned back to the Orient, to the first and eternal wisdom.—It seems that this is a dream of vulgar indolence!—Yet, I was not thinking particularly of the pleasure of escaping from modern suffering. I did not have in mind the bastard wisdom of the Koran. —But is it not a real affliction, that ever since that declaration of science, Christianity, man has been *playing,* proving his evidence, satiating himself with the pleasure of repeating those proofs, and living only in that way? Subtle, silly torture, origin of my spiritual wanderings. Nature can grow bored perhaps! M. Prudhomme was born with Christ." Ah! logic powerless to prove the excellence of the world!

Then down with the "vile education of my childhood," and let Eternity be compromised! "Then— ah!—poor dear soul, would not Eternity be lost for you?" If only the longed for *morning* rose on the world! "When shall we go over the strands and over the hills to salute the birth of the new labor, the new wisdom, the flight of tyrants and demons, the end of superstition, adore—be the first to adore—Christmas on earth?" Yes, but the "march of the peoples" has not yet begun, the hour has not yet struck, and those who, in a daring and indomitable effort, have tried to anticipate their time, are recalled to grim

149

reality. They say good-by to their chimerical dreams.

"Sometimes, I see in the heavens, endless shores covered with white joyous peoples. A great golden vessel above me agitates its multi-colored banners in the morning breezes. I have created all festivals, all triumphs, all dramas. I have tried to invent new flowers, new stars, new flesh, new tongues. I have hoped to acquire supernatural powers. Very well, then, I must bury my imagination and my memories! An artist's and story-teller's lovely aureole done away with!

"I! I who called myself magician or angel, exempt from all morality, am brought back to earth, with a job to look for and harsh reality to embrace! Peasant!"

And so, he is now nothing but a peasant. *Qualis artifex pereo!* He is now "brought back to earth," to "harsh reality." The absolutism which dominated his search for the ideal will also be affirmed in his energetic exploration of the real. To work! Adventure! But beyond all religious and moral conventions. Is not this renunciation a victory in its way? No more dreams! No more utopias! Live, humbly, strenuously, and that is all. Evil does not exist. Heaven does not exist. There is no sin, no baptism! Hell exists only in our minds: "I think I am in Hell, therefore I am." Let us be careful henceforth not to give over our souls to angels and devils, to make of it a field of battle, where they may engage in mortal combat! Let the weapons fall! Let us

150

abandon the "friends of death, the backward ones of all sorts!" To be positive, passionately so, therein lies salvation! "We must be absolutely modern. No hymns! Hold to the step we have gained!" Then, when the dawning comes, "armed with a burning patience, we shall enter into the splendid cities!" These are the last words of *Une saison en enfer!*

Rimbaud's mother read the book and understood not a word of it. It was, however, a striking proof of her own triumph. She had conquered her son. Rimbaud had killed the chimeras.

Dumbfounded, she asked him what these hermetic speculations meant. According to his sister Isabelle, his answer was, "I meant everything I said there, literally and in all senses."

It was better for him, however, that the book remained a mystery to his family. His exalted positivism grew out of the ruins of Christianity, and such implacable disbelief, in a young man of eighteen, would have scandalized all the godfearing people about him.

Paterne Berrichon, who pretends to have penetrated the arcana of *Une saison en enfer*, declares on the other hand that the poem is "the most profound, the most substantial affirmation of Christianity since the Gothic cathedrals, a poignant testimony of the reality of Catholicism." I don't believe this at all, and on this point I share the diametrically opposed opinion of M. Marcel Coulon. The *Saison* is for me an expression of the poet's last moral crisis and ends with "a rejection of God."

151

As simple as a virgin forest and as beautiful as a tiger, as Verlaine says, Rimbaud leaps with one bound beyond good and evil. In this sense, as Jacques Rivière has said, he seems "an innocent." He is no longer merely a bohemian, for the bohemian protests only against society. He protests against existence, such as it is, such as Christianity has made it. He feels himself anterior to redemption, anterior to sin—a pagan and a solitary. He has reëstablished contact with his primitive, Edenic origin. Rivière defines him as "the being exempt from original sin." Monstrous apparition in our world of compromise, of relativity, of half-measures and conciliation, he remains out of his element, like Shelley, inadaptable.

If he renounces literature ("to me only the story of one of my follies!") it is because he has violated her without success, it is because literature is incapable of carrying out his despotic and intractable demands; it is because, in this struggle with words and sounds, in the mad deformations of "the alchemy of the word," while practicing "the long, immense and reasoned disturbance of all the senses," he has stilled his inspiration and used up his genius. But at bottom he does not give up his absolutism. If he abandons it in literature, he retains it in his life. He remains loyal to his amorality, to his irreligion, to his implacable and archangelic pride, and, like Lucifer, bends neither before God nor men. He is amoral and atheistic. He can bear nothing, neither nourishment nor the propinquity of his fellow-men.

He becomes "a desert." *Une saison en enfer* is, in the strongest sense, "the poem of intolerance." Nothing can survive beside its flamboyant solitude. Its devouring blasphemy consumes all things: religion, philosophy, literature, poetry, prose. A unique adventure, Mallarmé used to say, in the history of the mind.[1]

He may have thrown a few copies of the *Saison* into the fireplace at Roche, which was dominated by a large crucifix; there is no reason for discovering any meaning, any symbolism in that gesture and that setting! Christ has not triumphed over the damned soul. Rimbaud is not converted. The flames have simply consumed his work. This is what he wanted: the void.

All about him, scattered on the ground, lie the dead bodies of chimeras! Like a young knight he has laid them low with his sword, on the edge of those pestilential forests whence his challenge had brought them. But he himself has breathed in the cursed air. He puts his hand to his heart and bends his head. Though victorious, he has killed himself. He has poisoned his own genius. His Muse is dead. He had launched himself into his amazing adventure like a madman, daring everything, overturning everything, destroying everything. He opposed his own gifts and acted in violence to his own inclinations. In order to be a "seer," he systematically used

[1] This is why his work is, according to the expression of Georges Duhamel, "a violent abbreviation of the history of literature." In three years he had passed through the entire literary evolution of modern times.

153

himself up. Alcohol, tobacco, hashish, lust combined to ruin him. Despite his exceptional and penetrating intelligence, he had clothed himself in obscurity. By weighing himself down, by shifting about, by bothering everlastingly about words, in silence and solitude, while renouncing the important corrections of the external world, he had weakened himself. In his exhausting researches for timbre and color, he had given himself over to the spell of "verbal hallucination." In his progress toward the impossible, he touched madness, and suddenly sobering, halted.

His poetry, like his life, is a tremendous transposition, a pathetic disguise. He experienced a satanic pleasure in exalting himself and destroying himself at the same time. He was the victim of his Lucifer-like pride, of his spirit of contradiction and revolt. Like a young Titan, he tried to scale the Empyrean. But he had scarcely engaged on the pathways leading up the mountain than he stopped to kill the Chimeras. His Muse died at his side, among his massacred dreams, in those vertiginous realms.

Then he descended from the lonely summit and threw himself into the tumult of cities, the deafening roar of railroad stations and of ports.

II

THE ADVENTURE IN REALITIES

La malédiction de n'être jamais las
Suit tes pas sur le monde où l'horizon t'attire.
                    —VERLAINE.

☆ I ☆

ACROSS OLD EUROPE

RIMBAUD's literary period is now over. The great adventure in ideas ended in a revolver shot. Another, more magnificent adventure begins, which will be pursued across several seas and continents. The intellectual instability of the poet will be transferred to the field of action. Only the medium is changed. There are not two different men in him; the adventure in realities is the same indefatigable wanderer, the same misanthrope, tenacious and closed, as the spiritual adventurer. Although he takes up another career, his attitude is unaltered. He remains consistent with himself. His concern now is to fight for a living, to explore the world feverishly. But in order to accomplish his desire one thing is necessary: a knowledge of languages. He must know English and German thoroughly.

In November, 1873, Rimbaud came to Paris. One evening he was seated at a table in the Café Tabourey, near the Odéon. The story of the Brussels drama and Verlaine's imprisonment was no longer

157

unknown in the "quarter." Tongues had wagged.
He was left strictly alone, as if in quarantine. The
touchy tribe of poets could not forget how merci-
lessly he used to jeer at them. There was whispering
and malicious laughter all about him. Suddenly a
young man with long brown hair detached himself
from a hostile group and came toward Rimbaud
with extended hand.

"Arthur Rimbaud?"

"I am he."

"I know of you. I have read your poetry. I would
like to talk with you."

The unknown who so publicly associated himself
with the outcast was the poet, Germain Nouveau, au-
thor of *Valentines* and *Humilis,* whose pathetic des-
tiny and lyric gifts have been made known to us by
Ernest Delahaye.

There was a striking contrast between these two
young men: the Ardennais—just nineteen, tall,
blond, gangling, his face child-like and ruddy; the
Provençal—twenty-one, stocky, black-haired Ara-
bian type, with a dull complexion, an aquiline nose.
The former was all bitterness, the latter all enthu-
siasm. Nouveau spoke of poetry. Rimbaud made
an evasive, discouraged gesture. Bah! Poetry no
longer interested him. Nothing was worth while but
travel, and as for him, he was on his way to Eng-
land. "When are you leaving?"—"Tomorrow."—
"I'll go along."—"All right, but it's going to be
hard. We'll have to earn our own living."—"So
much the worse. We'll manage somehow." No sooner
158

said than done, and a few days later they disembarked at London.

At first they were both employed by a box-maker. Later they gave French lessons. According to Ernest Delahaye, Rimbaud had returned to England with the definite purpose of perfecting his knowledge of English, knowing how indispensable that language is to a man who wants to go *everywhere*. How long did he remain in London with Nouveau? They seem to have separated rather soon, but not, as has been claimed, in consequence of a quarrel. Germaine Nouveau, less purposeful than Rimbaud, had quickly tired of vegetating, of looking for private lessons and ringing doorbells. Rimbaud found employment as a tutor in the British schools, first in London, later in the provinces, probably in Scotland. His stay in England lasted nearly a year, and when he had acquired complete mastery of the language he left for Germany, for once with his mother's consent and slight financial assistance, to acquire an equal knowledge of German.

At about the same time, in January, 1875, Verlaine was released from the Mons prison. In the course of these two years of meditation and solitude, he had renewed his allegiance to the Catholic Church. But he had not forgotten his friend of other days, and had arranged to send him a few poems, prison impressions like *"Dame Souris trotte......"* a religious effusion like the famous hymn *"O mon Dieu, vous m'avez blessé d'amour."* These had the result merely of exasperating the miscreant and they

159

were found later on in the latrine at Roche. With
the typical ardor of a neophyte, Verlaine longed to
bring the strayed lamb back to God. He wrote sev-
eral times to Ernest Delahaye to obtain Rimbaud's
address. Rimbaud was not at all interested in seeing
him again, but wearied by so much persistence, he
finally answered Delahaye: "I don't care. You may
give my address to the Loyola if you wish."

Three days later, Verlaine arrived at Stuttgart,
burning with fervor and apostolic zeal. Rimbaud
welcomed him with his usual sinister jeers, his cruel
and obscene banter, his familiar impieties and blas-
phemy. He took vicious pleasure in tempting him,
dragged him from brewery to brewery, getting him
thoroughly tipsy. In the evening, while they were
out walking in the suburbs, he engaged the drunken
evangelist in a discussion which speedily degenerated
into a fist fight. Since he was younger and more
athletic, he naturally got the upper hand, gave Ver-
laine a severe beating, and left him lying on the
banks of the Neckar, sleeping off the effects of his
beer. There was a reconciliation the next day. They
met again, but there was no more talk of religion.

Why in the world had Verlaine come to pursue
him? Why bring up these stale questions of poetry
and faith? All that interested him no longer. He had
come to Stuttgart to learn German. With this sole
intention he had engaged himself as a private tutor
in the home of a certain Dr. Wagner, which explains
—without seeing therein an apostrophe to the master
of Bayreuth—the inscription: *Wagner verdammt in*

Ewigkeit!—scrawled over a pencil sketch of a Stuttgart house in one of his letters. This is what he wrote Delahaye in February, 1875:

"Verlaine arrived the other day, clutching a rosary. . . . Three hours later, he had denied the Lord and made the ninety-eight wounds of our Saviour bleed again. He remained very reasonable for two and a half days, and on my advice returned to Paris, on his way to the island [1] to finish his studies. . . . I have only one week more of Wagner, and I regret this money paid hatefully, all this time wasted. On the 15th, I shall find me *Ein freundliches Zimmer*, any old place, and I shall whip away at the language frantically, to such effect that I shall be finished in two months at the latest."

There is no need, then, to imagine Rimbaud suddenly become music-mad, in turn enraptured and disgusted by the "music of the future," exhausting a Wagnerian "season" at Stuttgart as rapidly as he exhausts everything else. The reality is much simpler. He earned his living as tutor in the home of a German he detested, and had only one idea, to stay his month out ("only one week more of Wagner") and rent a room for himself in the city.

On his entreaty, his mother sent him fifty francs to permit him to wait for a new connection. "I have a very large room," he wrote to her on March 17th, "very well furnished, in the center of the town (Marienstrasse 2), for ten florins, that is 21 fr. 50 c., service included; and they offer me board for 60

[1] England.

161

francs a month. However, I don't need that; there is always some trick or drawback to these little arrangements, however economical they may seem. I am going to try then to manage until the 15th of April with what I have left (50 francs), because I shall need further advances at that time: either I shall have to remain here another month to make some progress, or I shall have placed some want-ads in the papers, and may need some money for traveling expenses to my job. I hope that you will find this moderate and reasonable. I am trying in every possible way to soak myself in the manners of these people; I am trying hard to learn, although one suffers frightfully from their kind."

However, at the end of four months at Stuttgart, his projects had not materialized. He did not find the situation he had spoken of to his mother, and the Württemberg "kind" enraged him as much as Prussian arrogance used to in Charleville, during the invasion. And then, after more than a year of tutoring in England and Germany, he was seized by the demon of adventure once again.

The maddening call of the road, the song of the unknown, intoxicated him. He sold his trunk to increase his resources, and left Germany. He went on foot toward the South, crossed Württemburg and Switzerland in high spirits, and arrived in Italy. This was the first time that he had set foot in the heroic land of the Cæsars and the condottieri. He penetrated into Italy by way of those perfumed valleys which open into the Lombardy lakes.

We have no record of his impressions of this visit. We know only that he arrived in Milan exhausted, worn out with fatigue and hunger, and that he had to take to bed. "There," writes Paterne Berrichon, "a signora, moved by pity, as well as charmed, one might almost say seduced by him, takes him in, cares for him—in short, shelters him for a month."

Is this tale correct? It has been seriously questioned. On the surface, it does not seem likely. Such voluptuous surrender to the delights of unexpected good fortune, such indolent relaxation, such gentle, though momentary subjection, are hardly consistent with Rimbaud's restless habits and quick impatience.

According to Ernest Delahaye, the episode had an altogether different character. The charitable Milanese, who lived at 2, Piazza del Duomo, was a cultivated old woman of the upper middle class, who cared for him in a motherly way. Attracted by his poor and yet talented air, she took him home with her and surrounded him with delicate attentions. He was not ungrateful, remembered her affectionately, and even sent her, in recognition, one of the few author's copies of *Une saison en enfer* that were still left to him.

Verlaine held the opposite opinion, and saw in the Italian woman a pleasant young widow whose hospitality was without restrictions. On two occasions he spoke of the "*vedova molto civile*" and associated with the story of this liaison the poem *Poisons perdus*

> *Des nuits du blond et de la brune*
> *Pas un souvenir n'est resté!*

163

Of the blond nights and the brunette
Not a single memory has remained!

There is only one difficulty with his thesis; that is
that these verses are not by Rimbaud, who wrote no
poetry after 1873, but probably by Germain Nou-
veau. Besides, how was Verlaine in a position to re-
ceive Rimbaud's confidences? At this time he in-
spired only contempt in Rimbaud, to whom his pious
fervor, his conversion, seemed an abdication, a de-
feat, a lot of mummery.

While he was in Milan, at the beginning of the
summer of 1875, Rimbaud suddenly decided to go to
see one of his friends, a soap manufacturer in the
Cyclades, and set out, on foot, on the road to Brin-
disi. On the way he had a sunstroke, and was sent
back to his own country by the French consul at
Leghorn. In Marseilles, his port of debarkation, he
made his living by performing the most menial tasks,
unloading trucks in the old port, helping the dock-
hands of the *Messageries Maritimes*, vegetating in
the busy seaport until he finally met a crimp of the
Carlist army who tried to get him to go to Spain.
It must have been a very brief enrollment, a passing
whim, since we find him in Charleville in October
1875.

At this date, he writes to his friend Delahaye, then
teaching at Rethel: "Received a postcard and let-
ter from V. a week ago. In order to simplify matters
I have asked the postoffice to forward all my mail
here (rue Saint-Bartholémy, Charleville). You may

164

write me here also, if you haven't already sent a letter to the other postoffice. I will not comment on the latest vulgarities of the Loyola, and I intend to do nothing about him at present, as it appears that the second 'portion' of the 'contingent' of the 'class' of 74 will be called on the 3rd of November following, or soon after."

What are these vulgarities of Loyola? They are the Catholic poems from *Sagesse*, that Verlaine persists in sending him through the intercession of Delahaye. Mercy! Can't he be left in peace? Poetry disgusts him, and religious poetry more than any other. He is already too far detached from literature to find any interest in Verlaine's productions, and for himself "has nothing more to do in that direction." Besides, the army is waiting for him. He has completed his twentieth year, is strapping, well-built, ripe for military service.

Rimbaud in a "képi" and red breeches! It is hard to picture this rebel performing automatically in the barracks courtyard or the parade ground. Fortunately, as his elder brother Frédéric is still in service (active service at that time lasted five years), he is exempt,[2] and plans to profit from this respite by working. Although he has renounced letters, he applies himself to the study of languages and the sciences. He learns Spanish, buys an Arabian grammar and dictionary, and plunges passionately into the

---

[2] This did not excuse him (according to a law then in force) from certain periods in the reserve. But he did obtain, by reason of his travels and his remaining abroad, frequently renewed stays, whose expiration always caused him great concern.

study of Arabian. In order to be free from interruption, relates M. Louis Pierquin, he would shut himself up in a huge cupboard, a kind of ancient chest, and there he would remain, often for twenty-four hours at a time, without food or drink. One day he would be studying Italian, another day Russian or modern Greek, Dutch or Hindu. He is indefatigable. All this work seems practical and necessary to him for the travels he means to embark upon. He has to have positive nourishment for his mind. Science and languages, these are the things that "help" in life, and he is ready, if need be—he who never wanted to take his degree in Rhetoric—to undertake the disagreeable task of new examinations.

In his letter of October 14, to Ernest Delahaye, he writes: "Do me this service. Tell me exactly and briefly what one needs for a science degree, classics, mathematics, etc. Tell me how far one must go in each subject, mathematics, physics, chemistry, etc. Also the approximate standards, and how one can procure the books used in your college [3] for example, for the degree, unless this differs in the various Universities?"

This winter of 1875, which Rimbaud spent at Charleville in studious idleness, saw Verlaine teaching in an English country school, finishing his hymns of *Sagesse* and his songs of repentance. Ah! if he could only convince his obstinate friend, convert him to his faith! "What do you say, wanderer through

[3] College Notre-Dame de Rethel, where Delahaye was the predecessor of Verlaine.

strange lands and ports, have you at least plucked *ennui*, since it is ripe?" He wrote Rimbaud in December: "I am always the same. Strictly religious, because that is the only intelligent and good thing to be. Everything else is deception, wickedness, stupidity. The Church has made modern civilization, science, literature, she has made France and she has made men—she *creates* them. I am surprised that you do not see this; it is so clear." And as Rimbaud on one occasion routs him with considerable loss and hubbub, "rubbish, potarada, etc.," he becomes saddened, and replies: "I longed so much for you to be enlightened and reflective. It is so painful to me to see you lost in these idiotic ways, you, so intelligent, so *ready* for it (although that may astonish you). I appeal to your disgust above all things, to your perpetual anger against everything, just anger at bottom, although unconscious of the underlying causes."

It is obvious, then, that Rimbaud had not already become a Catholic by 1873, when he burned his *Saison en enfer!* His renunciation of literature does not involve his adherence to Christianity. He quits the festivals of words and ideas, not the undertakings of the will, not the discoveries of human experience!

☆ II ☆

THE MIRAGE OF THE ORIENT

A T no time was Rimbaud more feverish, more unstable than during those years from 1875 to 1880. He crosses Europe rapidly in every direction and turns about dizzily. Unresting, purposeless vagabondage; madness of the highroads and the seaports. But stronger than all else, the Orient draws him on irresistibly, the barbaric, dazzling, everchanging Orient. Another vision, too, haunts him, of an unreal country where North and South struggle for mastery, where desert images mingle with visions of Babylonian cities. This is the same dreamy exoticism that used to haunt the nights of his *Enfance!* "This idol, black-eyed and yellow-haired," he wrote in the *Illuminations,* "without ancestry or attendants, is nobler than Mexican or Flemish mythology. Its domain, streaked with insolent blues and greens, includes beaches and shipless tides endowed with names ferociously Greek, Slavic, Celtic. At the edge of the forest dream flowers tinkle, burst, blaze forth —there is the orange-lipped girl, her knees crossed in the bright flood that springs up nearby, her nudity shadowed, crossed, clothed by rainbows, the flora, the sea."

And to recall his *Villes:* "Above the level of the highest crests, there is a sea troubled by the eternal birth of Venus, loaded with musical fleets and the sounding of pearls and precious shells; the sea darkens sometimes in deadly explosions. . . . The paradise of storms gives way. Savages dance ceaselessly the festivals of night. At a certain hour, I went down to join the turbulence of a Bagdad boulevard where troops of people sang of the joy of the new labor."

Although he has renounced translating these visions of mad, splendid incoherence into words, that does not mean that he is released from their magic. On the contrary, he is obsessed by them, the more so that they often remain unexpressed, the more so that he had driven back into the depths of his consciousness new and more daring images that begged for expression. But they lived on in the recesses of his mind and reacted on his will and his decisions without his perceiving them. Underneath his hunger for scientific knowledge and his most practical projects, one is aware always of the thrust of old longings.

Above all, beyond the roads, where the roads are broken off by the sharp line of the shore, the sea calls to him. Not the sad Northern sea nor the foggy gray Pas de Calais, but the Ocean of the *Bateau ivre,* with its "incredible Floridas" and "the yellow and blue alarm of the singing stars." Voluptuous sea, writhing under the golden caress of the sun, of that torrid sun that he has never really seen, that

169

he has never really gripped to his body in the surly
Ardennes or in damp England. All his travels hence-
forth will be stages in his progress toward the sun-
light, whatever detours life may force him to take.
Tireless Argonaut, even though he ships aboard a
vessel in some Northern port, Hamburg or Antwerp,
it is always in the hope of setting sail toward some
fabulous Colchis. His eye is fixed from afar on the
Golden Fleece.

To see foreign lands and to make money are twin
projects in his mind. He has the mentality of the
conquistadores. True, the unknown attracts him, but
he hopes to find also, in the silver-gilt horizons, a
kingdom with gold-bearing streams; he hopes to
trace the course of some new Pactolus. The reality
will be quite different: in order to earn a few francs
he will be forced to unload vessels on the shorefront
or work in a quarry on the Mediterranean coast.
He will try his hand at thirty-six different occupa-
tions: so many miseries! But no matter, he refuses to
become discouraged, comes back to France after each
trial to rest or recover from some illness. Then he is
off again toward the Orient.

In 1876 he shipped for Java; in 1877, on two
occasions, he tried to reach Asia Minor. The first
time he got as far as Austria, the second time he
fell sick on board and was set ashore in Italy. In
1879 and 1880 he was on the Isle of Cyprus, and
from 1881 on he traveled back and forth from one
side of the Red Sea to the other, from Asia to
Africa and back again.

The story of his first important voyage to the
Orient has been told in many different ways. The
simple version given by Isabelle Rimbaud is quite
inaccurate. According to his sister, "a Dutchman
of his acquaintance in London, an enlisted man in
the colonial army, induced him, by an enchanting de-
scription of the Island of Java, to go there with
him. In order to travel cheaply Rimbaud had him-
self engaged as a cabin-boy on the same ship that
his friend was on . . . etc." The truth is quite
otherwise: Rimbaud enlisted in the Dutch East In-
dian army and deserted as soon as he arrived in
Java.

Exact information on this exploit is lacking. Tire-
less walker that he was, Rimbaud probably went to
Holland by way of Antwerp. Strangely insensitive to
the delicate radiance of the landscape, to the bluish
wheeling of the windmills, to the pale play of clouds
in the sky and in the canals, he crossed the rich
plains and polders of Brabant and arrived in Rot-
terdam. There he must have wandered continually
about the quays, in the sailors' taverns, seeking in-
formation, inquiring about boats on the point of de-
parture. No favorable opportunity presenting itself,
he interviewed a recruiting officer who told him about
the impending departure of an infantry contingent
for the Sunda Isles. "They agree," writes Paterne
Berrichon, "and they go off together to the Helder.
There, for the sum of 1200 francs, 600 of which
were paid on signature, Rimbaud enlists with a troop
of Dutch soldiers about to set sail for the archi-

pelago." A Dutch critic has amended this slightly: our man, in reality, presents himself at the recruiting bureau of Harderwijk, on the southern coast of the Zuydersee, on May 19, 1876. In return for three hundred florins, he signs an agreement to serve six years. From there he sets out with a whole detachment for the port of the Helder, where he goes on board the steamer *Prinz van Oranje*. The boat sets sail June 10th.

We have no details of his voyage nor of the ports of call. Not a word has come down to us of Rimbaud's impressions of Bombay or Colombo. The Indian Sea no doubt seems less lovely to him than those of the *Bateau ivre*.

> *J'ai vu des archipels sidéraux! et des îles*
> *Dont les cieux délirants sont ouverts au vogueur!*

> I have seen sidereal isles! and archipelagoes
> Whose delirious skies are open to the traveler!

The voyage lasted six weeks, and on July 23rd the steamer dropped anchor in the port of Batavia. A torrid day. At the quay of Tanjong Priok, the long, repulsive buildings, docks, warehouses, customs offices, station houses, stretch themselves out under the burning sun. What a disappointment! Is this the miraculous and perfumed island of his dreams? This banal Dutch city, set down in a marsh like those of Holland, with rectilinear streets, shops set up soberly side by side, sad and dirty canals? Venturing into the Chinese kampong he just manages to dig up a few rare houses with beautiful red doors, three or four old buildings with convex roofs, decorated with fantastic animals and lacquered balconies.

Fortunately, all around the city, the luxuriant jungle vegetation triumphs. Cocoanut trees, banana trees, bamboos, arequiers, water palms with feathery leaves, parisiums with pale gold flowers, red parasol flaming—these are the trees of his dreams. Yes, but here too are the fetid, geometric barracks buildings at the end of an alley of waringins. He contemplates with intense disgust his blue cloth uniform trimmed with yellow. No, it was really not worth while escaping from service in France in order to come and be stupefied in Java! Dress parade, inspection and off to the brush he goes, his pack on his back. The volunteer is attached to the first infantry battalion quartered in the barracks of Salatiga, in the very heart of Java, 600 meters above sea level, on the slopes of Merbabu.

From then on Rimbaud's intention crystallizes: he will desert. He has achieved his aim. He wanted to see the Orient and the Orient has disappointed him. Discipline stifles him. He comes to hate these Dutch non-commissioned officers, these fat conceited blockheads who maltreat the natives. How much he prefers the society of the Malays, with their plain, coarse features, or the slender, muscular Javanese, with their oval dark-brown faces, their fearful and gentle regard! Strange beings, so attractive, so impenetrable also, strong and yet supple, immobile

173

and mysterious, a thousand times superior, in his mind, to the sluggish automatons of the barracks and the shooting-galleries. On August 15, 1876, at the end of three weeks of drill, of digging earthworks, of clearing the jungle and other drudgery, he manages to escape from the barracks of Salatiga and disappears in the forest. The sale of his civilian effects, left in a bundle in the company store-room, realized 1 florin 81 pence.

What became of him then? Did he wander over the neighboring plateau of Dieng, around the Indian ruins and the ancient temples? Did he cross through the forests of cocoanut trees to the old holy cities, to the sculptured pyramid of Broeder belted with Buddhic bas-reliefs, to the sanctuary of Brambanan with its multiple terraces, protected by one hundred and sixty sacred pavilions? Or did he scale the turbulent chain of volcanoes near there? Did he venture toward Papandayan, beyond the cultivated fields of tapioca and corn, across the gigantic and monstrous forests? Did he reach as far as those burnt cliffs, veiled by smoke arising from the sulphur beds? Did his bold foot tread the cracked and moving crusts of craters, with their poisonous crevices and pestilential fermentation? Who will ever know? It is probable, in any case, that he hid for a certain time in the heady thickets of the mountain, among the confusion of tree-like ferns, and that he descended finally toward the coast, passing rice plantations and ponds covered with water lilies, and reaching

174

Batavia finally after following the coast of the Javan sea.

Paterne Berrichon extends himself in order to give Rimbaud's desertion an heroic air. "In order to escape the barbarity of a military trial," he writes, "in order to escape being hanged, he was obliged to shun the Dutch colonials or civil officers, to hide in formidable virgin forests where the orang-outangs must have taught him how to save himself from tigers and from the surprises of the boa." No, Rimbaud did not have any such contacts, nor did he benefit from such a companionship.

There are no orang-outangs in Java, and, although there are some in Sumatra, it has been definitely proved that Rimbaud did not go there. Besides, the Dutch military code did not threaten him with capital punishment. It is far more likely that he traveled along the coast by short stages in the general direction of Batavia. He had got rid of his uniform, and one can picture him with the crowd on market day, mingling with Javanese dressed in flowered sarongs, with Sundian women, their hair dressed Chinese fashion, their backs bent under a load of rice bags or babies. By slipping behind the zebu-drawn carts, with their grinding wheels and their matted coverings, he gained the suburbs of the city, and once there, managed to reach the port by exercising almost Indian cunning. An English sailing vessel, carrying a cargo of sugar, was about to lift anchor. He signed as a seaman and departed for Europe.

175

La tempête a béni mes éveils maritimes . . .
. . . L'eau verte pénétra ma coque de sapin
Et des taches de vins bleus et des vomissures
Me lava, dispersant gouvernail et grappin.
Et des lors je me suis baigné dans le poème
De la mer, infusé d'astres et lactescent,
Dévorant les azurs verts ou, flottaison blême
Et ravie, un noyé pensif, parfois descend.

The storm has blessed my watery awakenings. . .
The green water has penetrated my hull of pine
And wine-blue stains and vomit of the sea
Have laved me, scattering rudder and grappling-hook.
And thenceforth I have bathed me in the poem
Of the sea, infused with stars and milky ways,
Devouring the green azures, where betimes
The pale and ravished water-mark of a drowned one,
Pensively descends.

The English boat suffered the same fate as the
Bateau ivre. "In the course of this voyage," writes
Paterne Berrichon, "two storms battered the vessel
about frightfully. Its sails split, its masts broken, the
ship was saved only at the cost of its cargo. Thus
disabled, they limped slowly and painfully around
the Cape of Good Hope, until they arrived within
sight of Saint Helena. Our deserter insisted on stop-
ping off here. The captain refused. Then, although
he was a poor swimmer, Rimbaud threw himself into
the sea with the intention of swimming to the island
made famous by Napoleon's captivity. A sailor, div-
ing after him, brought him back and got him on
board again by main force."

The authenticity of this adventure has been ques-

tioned. Rimbaud's known antimilitarism accords ill
with this gesture of passionate admiration for the
Emperor. The author of the *Rages de César* and
the deserter from Java would not seem, at first
glance, capable of such romanticism. But Rimbaud's
conduct is never a matter for easy prediction, and
his raging curiosity may very well explain this
stroke of madness. The story is also told by MM.
Bourgignon and Houin and by M. Louis Pierquin,
whose testimony is both faithful and conservative.
Verlaine knew it, having heard it probably from
Ernest Delahaye; he burst into laughter when told
of the adventurer's exploits, his dream of becoming
a trader. Parodying Rimbaud's accent, he recited
banteringly:

J'ai promené ma gueule infecte au Sénégal
Et vu Cinq-Hèle' (zut à Badingue) un' rud' noce.
Mais tout ca n'est pas serillieux: j'rêve eud'négoce. . . .

I have wandered to Senegal with my rotten jaw,
And seen Saint-Hell (down with Badinguet) a rough party.
But all that's nothing serious: I dream of business. . . .

However this may be, Rimbaud's travels do not
end with his return to European waters. He touches
at Liverpool, follows the coast-line of England and
Norway in another vessel, comes back by way of the
Dutch ports, goes south to Bordeaux, whence he re-
turns to the Ardennes on foot. He arrives in Charle-
ville on Saint Sylvester's day, December 31, 1876.

Thus terminates, in the snow and mist of the Ar-
dennes, this prodigious year, whose springtime saw

177

him in the flowering polders of Holland, and whose summer saw him in the forests of tropical islands. Eternal movement, eternal aspiration, eternal disenchantment!

At the first sign of good weather in 1877, he finds it impossible again to remain settled. The Far East proved a disappointment; but Asia Minor, Arabia, Persia still tempt him. How can he reach the Bosphorus and the golden gates of Asia? Under the pretext of rounding out his knowledge of German, he begs his mother to let him go to Austria, and extorts from her the price of a ticket to Vienna. From there he intends to go down the Danube, toward Varna and the Black Sea.

He arrives in the capital of the Empire in April, 1877. His first act is to take a carriage and treat the coachman to a few drinks. The coachman—in an exchange of favors—introduces him to some friends, two or three dubious characters who manage to steal Rimbaud's coat and pocketbook. Rimbaud is left on the street without a penny. He wanders about the terraces of cafés on the Ring, near St. Stephen's, half-beggar, half-peddler, selling keyrings and shoelaces, just as he used to on the Rue de Rivoli. Although our knowledge of the incident is not precise, we are not surprised to learn of his quarrel with a policeman. There is the usual procedure: abusive language, blustering, a gathering crowd, a scuffle, blows, wounds. He is arrested and expelled from the country as an undesirable alien.

178

Good-by, beautiful Danube, flowing toward the Levant! Our vagabond is not yet ready to follow you in your course!

The Austrian police conduct him to the Bavarian border, and from there, by virtue of a German order of public safety, he is sent under escort to the Lorraine border. He reaches the Ardennes by way of Montmédy. His second thrust toward the Orient has miscarried.

He sets off again, always on foot, toward Holland, and reaches Hamburg, where he hopes to find an opportunity to put to sea once more. But here he falls in with the Barnum of the period, the famous circus master Loisset, who needs an interpreter and barker for his tour of the Northern countries. Whatever the work, Rimbaud is never loath to use his legs. He makes the round of the fairs of Denmark and Sweden with this strolling troupe. Repatriated on his own request by the French consul at Stockholm, he comes back to Charleville the following September.

But he is possessed by a fixed idea: The Orient, the Orient! He leaves again for Marseilles where, after having earned some money as a stevedore, he ships for Alexandria. At the very beginning of the voyage he falls sick, and he is set on shore at Civita Vecchia. The doctor's diagnosis is gastric fever, inflammation of the walls of the stomach caused by the friction of the ribs against the abdomen, in consequence of excessive walking. (Verlaine rightly called him "the man with windy soles.") After he re-

179

covers, he goes to visit Rome, then comes back to spend the winter in Charleville.

His respite lasts but a few months, however, because he is still a victim of his obsession. The spring of the year 1878 finds him again in Hamburg, where he looks for employment with a company selling commodities to the colonies, but in vain. The following autumn, after the crop has been harvested at Roche, he travels again, by slow stages, toward the Mediterranean, haunted as always by the mirage of the Orient.

☆ III ☆

IN THE QUARRIES OF CYPRUS

WE are able to follow his course from the Vosges to Genoa in a long letter dated November 17, 1878. This is one of the rare documents that we possess on this period of transition, of gropings and of abortive beginnings, between his literary life and his commercial life, between Bohemia and business. It is an unaffected letter, but also without the surprising carelessness of his African correspondence, full of description that contrasts oddly with the dry tone of his ordinary family letters. One would say that he grants himself an instant of repose, that he takes a deep breath before throwing himself, body and soul, into the struggle for life and money. Later on he will disdain to tell of his really amazing travels and adventures; he will not describe Aden and its burning rock, nor Harrar and its high grassy plateaus. But here he tells minutely of mountain-climbing feats and the crossing of the Gothard pass.

"The road, which is only 6 meters wide, is heaped up all along the right side with a snow-drift nearly

2 meters high, which at any moment may deposit a barrier half its height across the road. This must be cleared despite a fearful sleet storm. There is this also: not a single shadow above, below, or anywhere around, although we are surrounded by enormous objects. No road is left, no precipice, no defile, no sky; nothing but white to dream about, to touch, to see or not to see, for it is impossible to lift one's eyes from the white torment that one believes is the middle of the path, impossible to lift one's nose to so biting a north wind. Lashes and mustache are stalactites, one's ears are lacerated, one's throat is swollen. Without the shadow that is oneself, and without the telegraph poles that follow this treacherous road, one would be as uncomfortable as a sparrow in an oven.

"Here we have a kilometer of road to trudge through with the snow more than a meter high. It is a long time since we have seen our own knees. This is hot work—for in half an hour the storm can swallow us up without much effort—we encourage each other by shouting. (No one goes through the mountain pass alone, always in bands.) Here finally is a food station; a bowl of salty water costs 1 fr. 50! Off again! But the wind rages more wildly, the road becomes blocked before our eyes. Here is a sledge train, one of whose horses has fallen by the way and is already half-covered over. We have lost the road. On which side of the poles is it? (There are poles on only one side.) We go astray (for a moment), plunge into snow up to the waist, up to the arm-pits.

"A pale shadow behind a trench appears; it is the Gothard hospice, supported partly by the Church and partly by the State for the purpose of rendering medical and other assistance to travelers —an ugly building of fir and stone. It has a small belfry. We ring the bell; the door is opened by a cross-eyed young man. We enter a dirty, low-ceilinged room, where they supply you free of charge with bread and cheese, soup and liquor. You can see the beautiful yellow dogs of the celebrated story. Soon those who have been delayed on the mountain begin to arrive, half-dead. In the evening, there are about thirty of us who, after supper, distribute ourselves on hard pallets under insufficient covering. At night we can hear our hosts express in sacred hymns their pleasure in stealing one day more from the governments that support their little hut.

"In the morning, after bread and cheese and a drop to drink, refreshed by that free hospitality that can be prolonged as long as one wants, we leave. This morning, in the sunlight, the mountain is marvelous; no more wind; the pass descends continually, over traverses, with jumps and slides kilometers long. We arrive at Airolo, on the other side of the tunnel, where the road again takes on the Alpine character, winding and obstructed, but all downhill. This is Ticino."

And above all there is sunlight. Rimbaud hastens toward Bellinzona and Lugano. There he takes

183

the train and goes on, by way of Como and Milan, toward the Ligurian coast.

There are no known facts about this trip, nor on his stay at Genoa. He embarks November 19th for Alexandria, where he arrives at the end of the month.

"I expect to find work very soon," he writes to his mother from Egypt, "as a matter of fact I am already earning enough to live meanly. Either I shall be engaged in a big farming project, about ten leagues from here, or I shall enter the Anglo-Egyptian revenue service at a good salary, or perhaps, and this is most probable, I shall leave for the island of Cyprus, the English possession, as interpreter for a gang of workmen. In any case, I have been promised something definite by a French engineer— an obliging and talented man—with whom I have been dealing."

However, in order to be taken on, he must present a certificate of good character, properly legalized by the local officials of his own country. He asks his mother to obtain this for him, to testify that "he has been working till now on her property, that he left Roche of his own free will, and that he has conducted himself honorably there and elsewhere." Here is a new Rimbaud, afraid to be taken for a vagabond, anxious to give guarantees, to show an official stamp, "above all the mayor's seal which is most necessary!" Times have changed since the day he used to insult burgomasters, judges, policemen. He is willing to show conformity even to the extent of a little lie. His mother must not betray him! It

184

is to her interest to become his accomplice in the deception as long as he has become serious, steady, and determined to earn his own living despite all difficulties. "Be careful not to say that I remained only a short time at Roche, because they will ask for a longer residence and the whole business will fall through. If you do that the people of the company will believe that I am capable of directing their workers."

After a stay of two weeks in Alexandria, he sets sail for Cyprus where he establishes himself, on December 16th, as a quarry foreman in the employment of a French company (Maison Thial, Jean et Cie.), at a salary of 150 francs a month. He writes from Larnaca, February 15, 1879:

"The contractors are at Larnaca, the principal seaport of Cyprus. I am supervisor of a quarry in the desert, on the sea-coast. A canal is under construction also. The stone has to be loaded on to the five sailing-boats and the one steamer of the company. There is also a lime-kiln, a brick factory, etc. . . .

"There is nothing to be seen here but a chaos of rocks, the river and the sea. There is only one house. No earth, no gardens, not a single tree. In summer the temperature is 80° (C.). At present, we often have 50°. This is winter. It rains sometimes. We eat game, fowl, etc. All the Europeans have been sick, except me. We have had twenty Europeans at the most in our camp. The first of

185

them arrived December 9th. Three or four of them have died.

"The native workmen come from the neighboring villages; we have employed as many as sixty per day. It is my job to oversee them; I assign the work and the disposal of the material; I make reports to the Company, keep account of the food and all other expenses, and act as paymaster."

Here he is then, a kind of foreman and overseer, living in a hut on the seacoast. He cooks his own food, does a little hunting along the coast, fishes and bathes in the sea. Does he know that only two leagues away, above the fields of buttercups and asphodels, the Gothic towers of Famagouste rear themselves among the palms? From Larnaca, the busy port where he delivers his loads of stones, the road goes directly to the City of Silence and Remembrance. What a vision for a poet, even for one determined to write no more, this old French city erected long ago at the brilliant door of Asia, and now sleeping forever within its feudal walls and its Venetian counterscarps! What an appeal it would have had for José Maria de Hérédia, what a spell it did cast over Gabriel d'Annunzio! Rimbaud was not even conscious of its existence. What cared he for those sculptured stones, those holy capitals spilled among the grass and the eglantine? What does that cathedral mean to him, abandoned like a great reliquary among the flowers? Why should he be moved by this melancholy splendor? The past, the past! He turns his back on it. He is busy handing out tools and weighing his charges of explosive.

"I am still head of the stone-cutters' yard," he writes on April 24th. "I charge and set off the explosives; I see that the stone is cut in the proper shape. The heat is very great. They are harvesting the wheat now. Fleas are a horrible torture, night and day. Mosquitoes too. I have to sleep on the sea's edge, in the desert. I have had quarrels with the workmen and I have had to ask for firearms."

As a matter of fact this cosmopolitan mob, which includes Greeks, Syrians, Arabs, Maltese, and even one Greek priest, is not always docile or manageable. In order to get the work done, Rimbaud must maneuver constantly, resorting sometimes to threats, sometimes to persuasion.

One day, a few of the men got drunk and pillaged his little house, stealing his cash-box. Rimbaud was greatly embarrassed, being left without the funds to pay his employees. Without permitting himself to be dismayed, however, he hunted up the guilty ones, appealed to their conscience and their honor, spoke of his own responsibility, of the injury they were doing to their comrades, and, after eloquent and diplomatic negotiations, succeeded in getting his money away from the, by now, sobered up drunkards.

One is amazed at the attitude he takes: it seems so incompatible with the legendary conception of Rimbaud! First he asks for a testimonial of good character, next he tries to convince sordid adventurers of the way of righteousness! In both cases he

187

was crafty, no doubt, calculating, playing a comedy, one might say. Yes, perhaps, but a certain lassitude, too, emerges from these actions. He is weary of sending forth his challenges to life. Life is stupid, deaf, does not understand. It strikes blindly, and does not value the heroic dreamer. Is it not better, then, to resign oneself, to manage to receive the fewest blows possible, to make the conventional gestures if they serve some purpose? The earthly adventure undoubtedly requires ardor, courage, daring, but it requires less absolutism, less intransigeance than the adventure in ideas. He must husband his strength, compromise with destiny on one point in order to realize advantages in other directions.

But in the battle of life, the stoutest heart is disarmed by the defection of the physical organism. At this time the weaknesses of a body enfeebled by excesses and further tried by an unhealthy climate begin to show themselves. This Cyprus springtime is torrid, oppressive; this sunlight (that he had sought everywhere) dries out the throat, sets fire to the eyes, empties one's brain. Rimbaud perishes of thirst in the white dust of the quarry, in the blinding reflection of the shore. The blood pulsates in his buzzing temples. He drinks some brackish water and is stricken with a fever.

He is forced to return to France. He disembarks at Marseilles in June, 1879, and has no sooner arrived at Roche than he goes to bed with typhoid fever. He recovers quickly, however, and makes himself useful around the farm, aiding his family, who, lacking tenant farmers, are themselves working the property where they mean to settle permanently. At this time, Ernest Delahaye comes to see him.

"He himself," writes Delahaye, "came to open the little rustic door at which I had knocked. An expression of great affection immediately spread over those features usually stiff with perpetual *ennui*. At first I could recognize only his eyes—so extraordinarily beautiful—the light blue iris surrounded by a darker ring of the color of periwinkle. The round cheeks of other days were now hollow, angular, hardened. His fresh rosy complexion—so like that of an English baby—that he had retained for so long, had been replaced by the dark coloring of an Algerian, and on this brown skin, much to my amusement, a tawny blond beard that had been slow enough in coming, made its appearance. . . . Another sign of his full physical virility was his voice, which, although hardly childish when I had last heard it, had had rather a nervous tone. It had now become grave, deep, full of a calm energy. Aside from this he was very gentle, working on the farm obediently, gathering in the harvest with the tranquil and methodical intensity of a lad who had never done anything else."

That evening, after dinner, Delahaye ventured to ask him if he was still interested in literature. "*I no longer think about it,*" he answered scornfully and irritably.

The next day the two friends took a walk around

189

the neighborhood. Although he described his life and hardships on the Island of Cyprus as a poignant experience, Rimbaud seemed to have every intention of returning there. The temperate regions were becoming too cold for him. Delahaye was amazed to see him shiver at the first autumnal winds, and reminded him of the long walks in the snow they used to take together. Rimbaud answered: "I couldn't do that any more, my constitution is changing. I must live in a warm country, at least on the shores of the Mediterranean."

Winter, in truth, was coming. He suffers from the biting wind from the Argonne, shivers in the mists of the Aisne valley, passes long hours cowering in the stable, near the sheep. Patience, patience! Life is not gay at Roche, his mother is proud and severe, as always, but it is warm, after all, in the stable, next to the mare Comtesse and old Father Michel, the Luxembourgian servant who takes care of the animals. And besides, while waiting to leave again for Cyprus and in order to mitigate the boredom of the winter season, he goes from time to time to "take a turn" in Charleville.

One evening—just before his departure—one of his friends, Ernest Millot, invited him to pass the evening with him and Louis Pierquin in a little café on the Place Ducale in Charleville. Rimbaud appeared, magnificently attired in a brand new suit. (He had bought the suit without his family's knowledge, asking the tailor to charge the bill to his mother.) When Ernest Millot congratulated Pier-

quin on acquiring a certain number of books pub-
lished by Lemerre, Rimbaud became very scornful:
"That's money thrown away. Buying books, and es-
pecially such books, is completely idiotic. You carry
a ball on your shoulders that should take the place
of all books. Books, ranged on shelves, only serve to
conceal the foul leprosies on old walls!" For the rest
of the evening he was unusually gay, overflowing
with good spirits. At eleven o'clock he said good-by
to his friends forever.

In the spring of 1880 he shipped for Alexandria,
going from there to Cyprus for the second time. On
this second visit we have no other information than
that given in a letter to his mother dated some time
in May. "I found nothing to do in Egypt and so I
left for Cyprus about a month ago. On my arrival I
found my old employers in bankruptcy. However, at
the end of a month I found the work I am now en-
gaged in. I am overseer at the palace being built for
the governor-general on the top of Troodos, the
highest mountain in Cyprus (2100 meters).

"I have been alone with the engineer up to the
present, in one of the two wooden huts that consti-
tute the camp. Yesterday fifty workmen arrived
and the work will now begin. I am the only overseer.
Until now I have had only 200 francs a month. I
was paid two weeks ago, but I have had a great
many expenses. I have to ride on horseback every-
where; transportation is very difficult, villages are at
great distances, food very expensive. Also, though
it is very warm in the plains, at this height it is still

191

and will be disagreeably cold for another month. It rains and hails, and the wind blows you off your feet. I have had to buy a mattress, blankets, great-coat, boots, etc."

In truth this Island of Cyprus is very inhospitable to him. The preceding year, on the shore or in the quarries of the plain, he suffered from oppressive heat. This time he is frozen on his mountain-top, in the midst of firs and ferns. "I am not feeling well, I have flutterings in my heart that annoy me considerably. But I'd better not think about it." The important thing is to find work to do and "to get good references," that will permit him to advance himself in the future.

Unfortunately his employment with the English administration on Mount Troodos lasts only up to the middle of June. Then he has to pack up his belongings again and go on to a job in a stone yard. But here too, things do not work out very well; he cannot get along with the engineer, has an argument with the paymaster, and finally decides to leave Cyprus and go to Egypt.

For the first time in his life he carries a small sum of money with him: 400 francs that he has saved himself.

☆ **IV** ☆

ON THE BANKS OF THE RED SEA

I HAVE looked for work in all the ports on the Red Sea, at Jidda, Suakim, Masgaua, Hodeida, etc. I have come here after trying in vain to find something to do in Abyssinia." In these words Rimbaud announces to his mother, on August 7, 1880, his arrival in Aden.

Will he remain here? How can he tarry anywhere? He is the victim of his own morbid instability. "When I have saved a few hundred francs, I shall leave for Zanzibar."

One can hardly blame him for wanting to quit Aden. Is there any place in the world more unpleasant to live in? Aden . . . in the month of August! Aden in the dog days! The harsh scene is transfigured in a magnificent horror. The black mountains bristle everywhere with iron cuttings. It is a mineral country. "Not a single tree, not even a withered one," he said later, "not a blade of grass, not a particle of earth, not a single drop of sweet water. Aden is the crater of an extinct volcano filled at the bottom with sand. There is absolutely nothing to see or to touch

193

except lava. . . . The sides of the crater prevent any air from entering, and we roast at the bottom of this hole as if we were in a lime-kiln. One must indeed be a victim of fate to work in such a Hell!"

Up above, at the end of the arena, and to the right of the Towers of Silence, there are great cisterns thousands of years old, hollowed out by an unknown race; they hold out their cyclopean vats and climb the mountain as if to approach the sky, as if to spy out miraculous clouds. In vain: they await eternally the storm that never comes. Everything is blazing. Not a breath of wind comes to freshen the torrid and suffocating air. At the edge of the metallic ridges, the English cannons crouch in motionless and sinister incandescence. The deceived brain receives images only of fire, and one can understand why the Arabs placed the smoking mouth of Hell here, in the Island of Sera. A Dantesque depression weighs on the soul. Only an accursed poet can live here.

Alas, the poet is dead. There is only an insignificant hireling left, a buyer for the house of Viannay, Mazeran, Bardey et Cie. "I am very well informed on the coffee market at present. I have the complete confidence of my employer. But I am poorly paid. I get only five francs a day, with board, lodging, laundry, etc., and horse and carriage, which amounts in all to about twelve francs a day." He worked, no doubt, in one of those low buildings strung out along the port, in the midst of bales of coffee and surrounded by Arabian porters. Every-

194

thing passes through his hands, he says, and he is "the only somewhat intelligent employee in Aden." However, he turns restlessly about, like a prisoner in a cage, in his "well-ventilated" office, where there is an even temperature of 40 degrees. Luckily one of his employers, M. Bardey, appreciates his worth, his resourcefulness, and sends him into the African territory to buy coffee from the growers. In his new position he is assigned to the office recently created by the firm at Harrar, which is the center of the important South Ethiopian market.[1]

In his letters to his family, Rimbaud is very sparing of details. "I arrived in this country," he writes on December 13, 1880, "after twenty days on horseback across the Somali desert." That is all. But we can easily follow him over the uncertain trail of the first caravans conducted thither by Europeans. At that time Ethiopia was still isolated; the mountains of Shoa and their foothills around Harrar were not yet connected with the coast by railroad. Jibuti was not even in existence. A small traffic was carried on between the little port of Zeila and the interior plateaux, subject to all the dangers and surprises of the desert. Rimbaud undoubtedly accompanied a caravan going back up into the hills. First of all one saw the straw-huts of the coast, then the immense gloomy expanse of ochreous land, with its volcanic stone and those large clumps of thorny mimosa from which would spring up, suddenly, a Somali warrior,

[1] Rimbaud was the third Frenchman to go to Harrar. His employer M. Bardey preceded him in August 1880 and left an assistant there who was succeeded by Rimbaud.

naked, armed with shield and lance. Then came the oasis of Biyo-Kaboba, the stopping-place of the caravans, where trees of unknown species are draped with heavy convolvulus and thick leaves, near the sandy bed of the spring, on which the tracks of a panther were still to be seen. Often the departure took place at night, on the small Abyssinian horses that fly like arrows and know how to avoid disturbing shadows. Finally, at the end of two weeks' march across this desert speckled with spiny thickets and dotted with cactus, marked, in fact, like a leopard's skin, after all this splendid and monotonous desolation, they reached the gentle ascent to the slopes of Harrar.

Here are locust-trees in blossom, tree-like begonias, fan-like ferns growing at the foot of gigantic sycamores that shelter, in the hollows between their roots, both zebras and caravanseers. The ascent becomes steeper, the horses fall behind the mules, and way up on top, the spurge, erect as a lamp-post, marks the road over the high plateaus. Turning around for a moment, one can see the Somali desert disappearing in the evening mist. We have left the domain of the nomads. Here, nearly 3,000 meters above sea-level, we are in the land of the shepherds. The zebus dream, buried in grass up to the dew-lap, and the Galla women emerge from their doors, carrying on their heads a tall jug of milk, like the amphora of ancient days.

Rimbaud will make this trip from the coast to Harrar many times in the course of the six years of

196

his association with the Aden firm. He will go back and forth from one end of the Red Sea to the other. He will become bored with it, as with everything, but for the moment, he is delighted with the contrast. He bathes himself voluptuously in the abounding vegetation of these mountains. And when, coming from the north, he debouches upon the ridge overlooking Harrar, a quick expression of joy comes into his astonished eyes. Here there is nothing of the aridity of Aden, the flat, unbroken line of warehouses and English barracks, strung along the coast, crushed by the leaden sky against the lava rocks. In its place we have a large Arabian city spread out among its gardens between overhanging hills. It bulges in its green basin like a watch glass set in a bezel of encircling walls and towered gates. The somber mass of hills circumscribes the tawny reddish vortex of its ten thousand buildings of dried brick. The terraced houses, arranged like the cells of a beehive, go off from the place of the mosque in a gyratory movement. From this circular disorder, only the minarets, crudely white, stand out against the blue sky, straight and slender, like lighthouses.

The caravan stops at the Turkish gate. It is a feudal entrance, flanked with bastioned turrets. An Egyptian military post is stationed there. A crowd of natives flock around as they enter the city. Rimbaud is welcomed by the local representative of the Aden firm, a former non-commissioned officer, who hands him his instructions, installs him in his office and puts him in possession of the agency which is on the principal square. He begins at 330 francs a month and M. Bardey promises him a percentage of the profits.

At first the business takes all his attention. With his prodigious power of assimilation, he soon commands the Harrar dialect. He buys coffee and musk, and sells cloths and glass trinkets. On market days the Galla women hurry in long files through the narrow tortuous lanes. On their veiled heads they carry wood, hay, pitchers of milk, jugs of water, bags of coffee. What do they find in exchange at Rimbaud's bazaar? Glass and china beads, colored handkerchiefs, printed cotton goods, and those little hand-mirrors so dear to their childish vanity. In the course of his many duties, Rimbaud makes frequent trips on horseback to the neighboring coffee plantations.

But soon his restless demon seizes him again. How can he remain long in this walled city? The Egyptian garrison—"a pack of dogs and bandits"—has turned it into a "sewer." Can he continue to live there in the midst of such putrefaction and excrement? Suppose he should one day follow—to its end —that river whose banks he has so often traveled on horseback, the Errer, which flows toward the Somali desert, across mysterious Ogaden—who knows—perhaps to the Aromatic Cape. He regards it musingly as it escapes out of sight. Where is it going? Toward what land of sunshine and perfume? Here in Harrar winter has come, and he shivers in the linen suit he has brought from Aden. In his letter to his mother he complains of the cold and rain—"and where are those woolen clothes that were ordered from Lyons months ago?"

By January 15, 1881, only one month after his arrival, the ambition to become an explorer supplants in his mind the goal of business success he had at first set for himself. Before leaving Aden, he had begged his family to have certain treatises on metallurgy and hydraulics sent to him, as well as practical craftsmen's guides, such as the manuals of carpenters, wheelwrights, tanners, glaziers, brickmakers, potters, "The Perfect Locksmith," etc. Now he asks for a "Theoretical and Practical Manual of Exploration." To be sure, he has his work to do; he must buy coffee, ivory, gold, perfumes, incense, musk and skins, all at good rates. But must he therefore sacrifice his liberty to this commerce, must he continue to live hemmed in by these drunken Egyptians and this abject population? On April 16th he announces to his mother the passage of some missionaries: "I may possibly follow them." May 4th he writes: "I expect to leave this town soon to make a trading expedition into the interior. There is a large lake a few days ride from here in the ivory country. I am going to try to get there." His projects do not mature. On May 25th, completely discouraged, he pours himself out in lamentations: "Alas! I have no interest at all in living; my portion is only fatigue. But if I have to go on this way and suffer such violent and absurd miseries in this frightful climate, I fear I shall not live long. If

199

only a man could enjoy a few years of real repose in this life! Fortunate for us that this life is the only one, and that that is evident, as one can hardly imagine another life more mortifying than this!"

While awaiting some change he goes back to his absurd and demoralizing labor. At least let some one help him make this hard-earned money productive! He sends 2500 francs to his mother: "Let this be safely invested in my name. It should yield interest regularly." His mother plans to buy "real estate." But no, he will not have it, what he wants is a reserve which will grow little by little and which he will find some day all ready for him when he returns. "What the devil do you want me to do with investments in real estate?"

The summer months come and pass slowly for him. However, "the coffee bushes are in bloom and they have a delicious perfume." O vanished poet, does this then move you?

At the beginning of the next year, he attempts to break away and returns to Aden to wriggle out of his contract. He plans to go on an elephant hunt in the region of those great lakes that lie farther to the south, in the mysterious heart of Africa. He intends to get a party together and even writes to a Parisian arms-house for catalogues. What attracts him above all is work of exploration. Even as a child at the Charleville College he had planned such exploits with his classmate in the fourth form, the future colonist Paul Bourde. Does he recall now the tales of the English travelers Speke and Grant which so stimulated his feverish adolescent fancy? Does he dream of discovering in his turn a negro kingdom resounding with war dances and war whoops, with a savage court and monstrous idols? Perhaps; but these plans of his youth are stripped now of their former romanticism in his letters home. He mentions nothing but documents and scientific instruments. He orders a camera directly from Lyons, and begs his mother to send on to his old friend Delahaye the following letter, dated January 18, 1882, Aden:

"I am about to write a work on Harrar and the Gallas, which I have explored, and submit it to the Geographic Society. I have spent a year in this country, in the employment of a French firm. I have just ordered a camera from Lyons which will permit me to illustrate my account with photographs of these strange regions. I lack certain instruments for making maps and I should like to buy them. I have a certain sum of money deposited with my mother in France, and I should like to make my purchases out of that.

"These are the things I must have. I should be infinitely grateful to you if you would buy these things for me with the advice of some expert, for example, a mathematics professor of your acquaintance. Go to the manufacturer of the best goods in Paris:

"1 A light transit. Have it carefully regulated and packed. The price of a transit is rather high. If it costs more than 1500 to 1800 francs, don't bother about it, but buy the two following instruments in-

201

stead: a good sextant, and a surveyor's level.

"2 Buy a minerological collection with 300 samples. This is a common commercial article.

"3 A pocket aneroid barometer.

"4 A surveyor's plumb line.

"5 A draughting outfit, including a ruler, a square, a protractor, a proportional divider, a scale, a ruling pen, etc.

"6 Drawing paper. And the following books:

"*Topographie et géodésie*, by Commandant Salneuve (published by Dumaine, Paris).

"A Trigonometry used in advanced college courses.

"A Minerology used in advanced college courses, or the best text-book of the Ecole des Mines.

"Hydrography; the best text-book you can find.

"*Météorologie*, by Marie Davy (published by Masson).

"*Chimie industrielle*, by Wagner (published by Savy, rue Hautefeuille).

"*Manuel du Voyageur*, by Kaltbrünner (published by Reinwald).

"*Instructions pour les voyageurs preparateurs* (published by the *Librairie du Muséum d'histoire naturelle*).

"*Le Ciel*, by Guillemin.

"Lastly, *l'Annuaire du Bureau des Longitudes* for 1882.

"Make a list of all your expenditures, add your own expenses, and pay yourself out of the funds I have deposited with my mother in Roche."

202

But he reckons without his mother's customary rapacity. A transit, a camera, what expensive foolishness! Mme. Rimbaud, of her own initiative, has invested his savings of 2500 francs in real estate. The letter addressed to Delahaye she keeps for herself. She knows these extravagant moods! In a new guise, they are the same devouring whims that he had had before. Formerly he had a mania for writing and traveling. Now he has an abnormal passion for the sciences. Will her son never learn? How fortunate that she is there to put a stop to such wastefulness! What is the use of earning good money just to throw it away on books? . . . which might never reach him anyway? To be sure, he had just sent her another sum of a thousand francs, but the camera alone—the boy must be crazy!—cost 1800 francs. No, it is time some one spoke to him clearly and firmly, once again. . . .

And Rimbaud receives a letter full of angry chidings and recriminations. So his money has been converted into land, against his will, and he must renounce his scientific projects, his geographical work, his dream of becoming an explorer? Come then, take up your chain and ball again, cast your eyes on the ground, go on your weary way forever! The unhappy man renews his contract. He hasn't even the courage to protest: the tone of his letters to Roche is sad, entreating. He writes from Aden, December 8, 1882:

"The most melancholy thing about your letter is that you end by saying that you will have nothing more to do with me. That's a nice way to help a man thousands of miles from home, traveling among savage peoples and without a single correspondent in his own country! I am sure—I hope—that you will not persist in such an uncharitable intention. If I cannot ask even my family to do things for me, who the devil should I ask? I lately sent you a list of books I wanted to have. Please don't send my requests to the devil!"

At the beginning of the year 1883 then, he returns to Harrar. He evidently harbors no resentment against his mother, as the first photographs he makes are intended for her. One shows him "standing on the terrace of his house," another, standing in a field of coffee, a third, "in a grove of banana trees, his arms crossed." (Was that the "tragic" picture that Claudel beheld with so much emotion one day at Roche, and in which Rimbaud appeared "black as a negro, bare-headed, barefoot," dressed like a convict?)

And now war breaks out between Egypt and Abyssinia. The business is threatened with disaster. Harrar draws itself together, contracts within its tawny walls. The terraces of its houses are deserted. The whole silent city is on guard. The gates are closed. Rimbaud—he who loved so to be alone—suffers now from loneliness. It is profoundly moving to see this proud man weaken. At first he had wanted to defy life, then overcome her, conquer her. Life was stronger than he. Now he wants only to bargain with her, to get his daily bread and a corner to rest in.

He who used to flaunt his rebellious individualism in the face of society now complains—like so many others—that he has no home, no family. He writes from Harrar, May 6, 1883:

"Solitude is a frightful thing here, and I am sorry I am not married and have no family of my own. For the present, attached as I am to this distant enterprise, I am condemned to wander, and every day, more and more, I lose my taste for the climate, the ways of living, and even the language of Europe.

"Alas! What is the use of all these goings and comings, these fatigues, these adventures among strange races, these languages with which I fill my memory, these nameless griefs—if I cannot some day, after a few years, find repose in some pleasant spot, and raise a family? At least I should like to have a son, whom I could spend the rest of my life bringing up according to my own ideas, giving him strength and accomplishments by means of the most complete education available in our time, and whom I could see becoming a celebrated engineer, a man made powerful and rich by science? But who knows how long my days will be, in these mountains? I could disappear in the midst of these peoples, and the news might never reach the world.

"You write to me of political events. If you only knew how little I cared about such things! It is more than two years since I have looked at a newspaper!

205

All those controversies are incomprehensible to me now. Like the Mohammedans, I know that what happens, happens, and that is all. . . ."

Fortunately this fatalism does not sap his energy. These fits of depression are as transitory as they are frequent. The necessity for immediate action leads him away from his revulsions and regrets. The exploration that he wanted to attempt on his own responsibility meets with the approval of his employers in Aden, and it is with their authorization and support that he will confront the mysterious desert.

☆ V ☆

THE EXPLORER

I F one looks over the Bulletins of the *Société de Géographie* from 1880 to 1890, one finds frequent allusion, in the reports of the general secretary, to the African explorations of M. Bardey. The latter was only, as a matter of fact, a plain business man. However, he had a cultivated and curious mind, and saw beyond his immediate business interests. He knew how to take advantage of Rimbaud's daring and tenacity for the advancement of science. He encouraged Rimbaud from his office in Aden, and, whenever it was necessary, consoled him and kept up his spirits.

Besides, at a time when business was very inactive in Ethiopia because of the war with Egypt, he thought it expedient to give his agent something to do, to direct his activity toward the unknown deserts of the South. On November 24th, 1883, he wrote to the *Société de Géographie,* of which he was a member:

"M. Rimbaud now has charge of all our expeditions into Somaliland and the Galla country. The

exploration of the Wabi region, in the Ogaden coun-
try, is entirely due to him. You are probably aware
of the fact that in a similar expedition M. Sacconi,
an Italian explorer, lost his life. M. Sottiro, our
agent, was held prisoner for two weeks and was not
released until after M. Rimbaud had sent an Ogas,
or chieftain, from Harrar to secure his liberty."

The year 1883—Rimbaud's third year spent out-
side of Europe—was in fact distinguished by daring
explorations. He was the first European to go from
Harrar to Bubassa, a large plateau about 50 kilo-
meters south of the city, where he remained for
over two weeks and established commercial rela-
tions. Then, encouraged by his success, he extended
his surveys to the southeast, drew them out along
the rivers which came down from the mountains
of Harrar and disappeared in the direction of the
Indian Ocean. By following the river Errer, he ar-
rived at the Ouabi or Wabi river and penetrated into
Ogaden.

Ogaden is a country of shepherds, nomads and
warriors, almost entirely without villages or roads, a
completely unknown desert at that time (the Ger-
man, Hagenmacher, had tried in vain to penetrate
into Ogaden in 1875), and to tell the truth, but
little explored since. Fifteen years were to pass be-
fore a few European aristocrats, big-game hunters,
were to venture there. Ogaden offered them marvel-
ous resources for their princely hunts, and reserved
sensational surprises. Already in 1883 Rimbaud had
discovered, on the banks of the Wabi, "all the ani-
208

mals of the great rivers, elephants, hippopotami, crocodiles," without counting "wild animals of the commoner varieties . . . gazelles, antelopes, giraffes and the rhinoceros, whose skin serves as a shield for the natives."

As for Rimbaud, his ambitions were both more modest and more scientific than those of the big-game hunters, and one is struck, in reading his short report to the *Société de Géographie*, by the deliberate dryness of his tone, the strict and bare precision of his account. The adventurer has disappeared; it is the geographer who writes now.

"The general aspect of Ogaden is marked by a steppe covered with high grass, interspersed with rocky chasms. The trees, at least those in the region explored by members of our party, are all those of the Somaliland desert, mimosa, gum-trees, etc. However, as one approaches the Wabi, the population is settled and agricultural. They cultivate *dourah* almost exclusively and even employ slaves who are natives of the Aroussis and the other Gallas from beyond the river. . . .

"The people of Ogaden, at least those whom we saw, are tall, and generally reddish in coloring rather than black. They go about bareheaded, cut their hair short, wear rather clean clothes, carry the *sigada* on their shoulders, a saber and a gourd for water on their hips, a crook and a large and a small lance in their hands, and sandals on their feet.

"Their daily occupation consists of going some distance from the encampment and squatting down,

209

fully armed, in groups under the trees, there to deliberate vaguely upon their various interests as shepherds. Aside from these meetings and occasional patrol duty on horseback, while their neighbors are watering their stock or raiding each other, they are completely inactive. The care of the animals, the manufacture of household utensils, the building of huts, the management of the caravans, are all left entirely to the women and children. Their utensils are vessels for holding milk like those seen in Somaliland, and camel's hair matting, slung over sticks, form the houses of their temporary dwelling-places. A few smiths wander about among the tribes and forge their lance-heads and poniards. . . . The people of Ogaden are fanatical Mohammedans. Each camp has its *iman* who calls the faithful to prayer at the proper hours. *Wodads* (learned men) are found in every tribe; they know the Koran, can read and write the Arabian script, and are extemporaneous poets of a kind."

Poets? And he? Ah, he is less a poet than these learned men of the desert. He has lost even his taste for dreams. And how should he find time for them? He is much too busy equipping his caravans, preparing his wares for barter with the natives, running down tribes that are known to possess much ivory. His interests are elsewhere than in poetry: these savages have ivory to sell him—is not that the most important thing? "The Ogaden men hunt on horseback. While about fifteen of them engage the elephant in front and at the sides, an experienced hunter cuts the hindermost hamstrings of the animal with his sword. They also use poisoned arrows."

Rimbaud wrote this report December 10, 1883,[1] on the return of his assistant, the Greek, Sottiro, who seems to have penetrated deeper into the country than he. Sottiro reached as far as Galdoa, a point which, according to M. Bardey, had not yet been exceeded in 1901; but as the letter cited would indicate, he nearly failed to return at all. The aborigines seized him and threatened to put him to death, until Rimbaud despatched to them one of his friends, the Ogas or oughaz of Malingur, the most powerful chief of upper Ogaden, who obtained his release.

The caravan returned to Harrar then without any loss. One can imagine the joy and pride of Rimbaud when he saw his companion return exhausted but beaming. He was able to feel that his efforts on behalf of the other man had not been in vain. For the first time in a long while he was returning from a leap into the unknown without a bitter and disappointed smile. He had penetrated deep into the desert and had found something other than a mirage. His camels brought back ivory, rhinoceros and crocodile skins. He and his men had gone farther along these adventurous trails than any other European.

The *Société de Géographie* thanked him for his

---

[1] This report did not pass unnoticed, and in 1884 was declared "of great interest, despite its dryness," by the Austrian geographer Philippe Paulitschke who continued Rimbaud's explorations in Ogaden in 1885 and 1886.

report on February 1, 1884, and "wishing to make a collection of the pictures of persons who had made a name for themselves in geographical research and travel," asked for his photograph, "the place and date of his birth, and a brief statement of his works."

His works? He has none to name. The most he could do would be to enumerate the titles of his poems, supposing that he still remembered them. Bitter reminder of the past, irony of destiny! Paris had forgotten the author of the *Bateau ivre*. Would she be interested in the explorer?

Rimbaud did not answer.

At this very time, anyway, his career as an explorer was ended. In consequence of business reverses, the Aden firm was forced to liquidate. The Harrar agency was discontinued, and Rimbaud recalled.

Once more he sets out for the coast. It is not without some melancholy regret, despite the irritations and the cares of his position, that he leaves the perfumed coffee fields, the swarming, motley-colored alleys, the large low house where antelope skins, ostrich plumes, elephant tusks lie heaped up together with Italian glassware and Lyonnaise silks. He says good-by to those swift rivers ever in flight toward Ogaden, its sands and stones. No more will he gallop across the golden steppes, nor hunt the hippopotamus on the banks of the Wabi, nor sit in the shade of the gum-trees in "kalamas," or endless conferences with the thieving Somalis. Now he must return to the fiery furnace and an uncertain future.

212

On the way to Zeila, he carries along with him in his belt 40,000 gold francs,[2] and in the evening, in his tent, lying on his bed of goat-skins, within instant reach of his rifle, he is on the alert at the slightest noise, the footsteps of the camel-drivers in the shadows, the rustling of the clusters of mimosa. . . . He arrives finally at Aden, wanders along the burning wharves, by the warehouses, without employment. "What a deplorable existence," he cries out, "I lead in this absurd climate, and under what frightful conditions! How boring! How stupid life is! What am I doing here? And what should I look for elsewhere?"

Finally, in June, 1884, after the affairs of the corporation have been liquidated, M. Bardey takes over the business and asks Rimbaud to come back to work for him. Demoralized and nervous, Rimbaud had, in the meantime, established a temporary home for himself. The author of the *Petites Amoureuses* (O memories of Baudelaire!) lives with an Abyssinian woman:

> *Cheveux bleus, pavillon de tenebres tendues*
> *Je m'enivre ardemment des senteurs confondues*
> *De l'huile de coco, du musc et du goudron. . . .*

> Blue hair, pavilion of strained shadows,
> I'm drunk with rapture at the mingled perfumes,
> Of tar, of musk, and of cocoanut oil. . . .

[2] M. Marcel Coulon, in an article published in the *Mercure de France,* March 15, 1929, claims that the letters from which these figures were quoted had been improperly transcribed by Paterne Berrichon, Rimbaud's brother-in-law and biographer. The sum with which Rimbaud traveled through Africa was not forty thousand francs, but from twelve to fifteen thousand francs.—*Tr.*

Did he bring her back with him from Harrar?
Perhaps. The only information we have on their life
together comes to us from M. Bardey's servant,
Françoise Grisard, who used to give the African
woman sewing lessons.

"It is true," she writes, "that I used to go almost
every Sunday after dinner to M. Rimbaud's house.
I was even astonished that he permitted me to come
there. He would say very little. He seemed to me to
be very kind to this woman. He wanted her to learn.
He used to say that he would like to send her for
a while to the nuns, at Père François' mission, and
that he wanted to get married because he meant to
go back to Abyssinia, and that he would never go
back to France unless he had made a large fortune.
He used to write a good deal; he told me that he
was preparing some fine works.[3] I do not know how
I learned that all his books and papers had been de-
posited with Père François: I must admit that my
memory has been failing me for several years. As for
this woman, she was very gentle, but she spoke so
little French that we could never really talk to-
gether. She was tall and very thin: had a rather
pretty face, with regular features, not too black. I
do not know the Abyssinian race; to my mind she
seemed quite European. She was a Catholic. I do
not remember her name. For some time her sister
stayed with her. She went out only in the evening,
with M. Rimbaud. She dressed in the European

[3] Apparently the reports for the *Société de Géographie* or ac-
counts of his travels.

214

style, but their home was exactly like that of the people of the country. She used to enjoy smoking cigarettes a great deal."

Around this time, Mme. Rimbaud tried to induce her son to return to France. He refused. "In France I should be a foreigner and I should get nowhere," he wrote at the very time that the Symbolists were making a great to-do about his work. And then, it seemed impossible for him to readjust himself to European life. He was completely uprooted, and, as someone has said since, decivilized. But further, he would die of cold and misery if he had to go back to country life in Roche, in those disagreeable, gray Ardennes! He answers his mother, January 15, 1885:

"If I had the means to travel without being forced to remain in any one place, if I could work and earn a living, you would not find me in the same place more than two months. The world is full of magnificent places that could not be visited within the lives of a thousand men. But on the other hand, I should not like to be a miserable vagabond. I should like to have an income of a few thousand francs and be able to spend the year in two or three different countries living modestly and doing some interesting, intelligent work. Living always in the same place would make me very unhappy."

His chronic instability, his perpetual need for change and renewal, inherited no doubt from his father (and sometimes called an ambulatory paranoia), explains the disgust and horror he soon be-

gins to feel for his life in Aden. His personal life
(I do not dare speak of it as domestic happiness)
also languishes in this torrid prison. He is not satis-
fied with having gratified his senses in this uncon-
ventional way, a way which may seem to him some-
what humiliating for a man of his type. Behind his
counters, among the cases and sacks of his ware-
houses, does not his liberty languish too, all bound
and stifled? He is disgusted with the shopkeeper's
and salesman's existence, the barren and monoto-
nous days. Dreary commerce, high cost of living,
privations, what is there in it all for him? "Every-
thing is very expensive. I drink absolutely nothing
but water, and that costs me 15 francs a month.
I never smoke, I dress in cotton cloth . . . I take
no newspapers, there is no library. As for Euro-
peans, there are only a few idiotic commercial em-
ployees who spend their whole earnings at billiards
and afterwards quit the place, cursing it." Ah! if he
could only take flight himself, go to India, to Ton-
king, to the Panama Canal! For mercy's sake, a cool
breath of air, a wider horizon, a little altitude!

The high plateaus call him again. Pastoral and
savage pictures pass through his overheated mind.
In his nights of insomnia, the limitless horizons of
Ogaden rise like a mirage; the Abyssinian moun-
tains appear in a violet mist, and in the depths of
his vision he can hear the dusty tread of caravans.

☆ VI ☆

THE CARAVAN TO MENELIK

I HAVE thrown up my job in Aden after a violent
quarrel with those mean upstarts who would
simply choke me up all my life . . . I have sent for
a few thousand muskets from Europe. I am going
to make up a caravan and carry this merchandise
to Menelik, king of Shoa." It is in these decided
terms that Rimbaud announces his departure for
the coast of Africa, October 22, 1885.

At the beginning, he is full of optimism and self-
confidence. On November 18, he writes, "I am glad
to leave this frightful hole (Aden), where I have
suffered so much. I confess that the trip I plan is
arduous. From Tajura to Shoa, I have fifty days
of travel on horseback through the burning desert.
But in Abyssinia the climate is delicious: it is neither
hot nor cold, and the population is Christian and
hospitable. Life is very pleasant there. It will be
especially agreeable for me to rest there after years
of sheer prostration on the sweltering shores of the
Red Sea." He asks his mother to have the diction-
ary of the Amhara dialect sent to him. Then he set-

tles himself for a while at Tajura, annexed but recently to the French colony of Obock, in order to set up and equip his caravan on the spot. He has planned his transaction carefully, there seems to be no hitch, and he hopes to make 25,000 francs clear on his expedition.

However, the expedition involves considerable risk and danger. To reach Ankober, Menelik's capital (Menelik is not yet King of Kings, but king of Shoa and vassal of the Negus of Abyssinia) he must make his way across the desert between the ill-defined territories of two hostile tribes, the Adali, of the Danakil or Dankali family, and the Aussa, of the Somali family. Tajura at this time is only a little Danakil village, built at the foot of volcanic mountains, consisting of one or two mosques, a few palm-trees, brownish-yellow straw huts and one brick hut where six marines sleep all day long.

Rimbaud's preparations drag along for months. The natives he engages leave him one after another. He finds it impossible at first to obtain camels. But worse, the expedition is undertaken at a most unpropitious time. The Danakils along the coast had just assassinated the crew of the coast survey boat, *Pingouin*. A caravan, directed by another Frenchman, Barral, was massacred in March, 1886, half-way between Shoa and the sea, and a friend of Rimbaud, M. Chefneux (later French consul-general in Ethiopia), going back over the scene, found only some scattered guns and corpses half-devoured by hyenas. All this is not very reassuring. Ever since

England forced the Negus of Abyssinia to abolish the slave trade, the natives detest all Europeans equally. The white man is more than ever their enemy. He has ruined their most flourishing trade, and in revenge they spy on him, from the mountain defiles, along the rivers, at the edge of oases, to plunder and slaughter him.

Of these nomadic and warlike tribes, Rimbaud fears most of all the Danakils. The Aussa are well known to him; he knows their language; he has met them frequently in the preceding years on the Somaliland trails and even in the market-place at Harrar. The others are more troublesome; they are fanatical and cruel Bedouins. Thin, nervous, with kinky hair, adding to their height cunningly by means of large combs, they wear no other clothing than a pair of cotton drawers or a cotton cloth wound around their hips. With naked torsos, a round shield on their elbows, a dagger at the waist, they pounce unexpectedly on passing caravans, brandishing their lances and uttering their fierce war-cry. Decidedly these Danakils promise him no easy passage!

However, he is not the kind of man to retreat. But if only he had nothing but savages to fear! Other cares threaten to overwhelm him. His partner, Labutat, a French business man of Shoa, falls gravely ill and goes back to France to die of cancer. Rimbaud therefore has to assume alone all the obligations of the partnership, and go on with the proposed enterprise without any assistance. Finally,

219

to complete his bad luck, his friend, the explorer, Soleillet, who had already gone over the route and was to have accompanied him, dies suddenly at Aden, September 9, 1886.

Is there a warning of Destiny in all this? Should he give up? The look of defiance that we know so well appears in his keen eyes. No! The order is to march. After countless annoyances, endless dealings with natives, guides, with Arabian camel-drivers and Abyssinian muleteers, the caravan is made ready, and encamps under the palm-trees of Tajura. On the command of the chief, they set out toward Shoa around the middle of December.

At first there is a gentle ascent, over heaps of rubble-stone, toward the high plateaus of the interior. Dry, burning soil, with here and there a stunted gum-tree among the burning rocks. Not a single spring, not a single well. Soon a halt is called. What a strange picture! An amphitheater lies hollowed out before the caravan. Dazzling and congealed, a sheet of hard blue water, like a steel mirror, is spread in the gloomy setting. Lake Assal lies peacefully in its basin well below the level of the sea. The wide white border all around it is salt. The caravan descends to the valley among the spurge, the aloes, and other rank growth. They set up camp on the banks of the lake which seems hemmed in with petrified foam. The salt deposit attracts the camel-drivers who collect as many of the snowy crystals as they can to sell to the mountain people of Shoa.

As they continue on their way the aspect of the country begins to change. The caravan must mount up the other side of the lake basin along the bed of a river. The trail follows through a narrow pass overhung by great blocks of porphyry. On both sides, the route is lined with grottoes. The camels advance with difficulty. The gorge opens finally upon the plateau, at a place called Koido. The tents are set up, fires are lit. In the distance the war-cry of the Danakils echoes in the moonless night. There are frequent alarms. The men leap to their guns. Low groans, muffled lamentations are heard. Fear seizes the camp. Then the desert subsides into silence.

From here, either of two trails can be taken, and Rimbaud consults with his camel-drivers. Should they follow the route to the left, which cuts through the Aussa territory, or should they embark resolutely on the road to the right, within the zone of the Danakils? The tribe that massacred Barral's caravan will not hesitate to repeat their exploit. They are probably on the lookout, hoping to meet with the "franghi" (Frenchmen), somewhere. The conference is protracted endlessly, and so Rimbaud, prudent when necessary, decides for the route to the left. It seems wiser to him to inspire confidence in his frightened and jabbering men, victims of their overwhelming fear of the desert night, than to gain time on the other route.

After a month of traveling across the immense bare plateau, traversed occasionally by an antelope in flight, the caravan arrives at Errer. Wretched little straggling village—the first met with since their departure—on the boundary line between the territories of the two tribes. About twenty of the huts in the village belong to the Danakils, twenty others to the Aussa. The former execute their war-dance before the caravan as a sort of challenge. Without paying any attention either to their challenges or their bravado, Rimbaud goes further on and sets up his tents on the further edge of the village.

And the journey continues, monotonous, back-breaking. On his small Abyssinian horse, his loaded pistols in their holsters, his rifle hanging across his chest, the chief brings up the rear. As far as one can see, the high volcanic plain stretches out with not a single tree on it. On two occasions the caravan hastens forward: in the west marvelous mountains are reflected in rippling waters. Alas, as they approach, the illusory lakes disappear. A sand storm comes up and whirls about them. The mirage fades. The eyes of the travelers burn with the stinging sand. Will they never arrive at their destination?

Finally the level of the land becomes lower. At 800 meters altitude, the river of Shoa, the Hawash, cuts through its deep valley. The caravan crosses it at a ford; here they have left the region of danger and ambuscade behind. Here ends the sway of the nomadic tribes and the kingdom of Menelik begins.

These last stages of the ascent toward Ankober are so exhausting! They mount from 1000 to 3000 meters above sea level. The animals suffer frightfully in the narrow, rocky passes. There is a halt at Farré, the first Amhara village. Here everything is different, the people are curious and hospitable. The natives have been expecting the caravan: for days past they have been seeing its fires in the plain. The packing-cases are opened, and the women crowd around the dress-stuffs and the glass bead necklaces. Seated on a cowhide in front of his round hut, made of boughs and topped with a conical roof of thatch, the Amhara chief receives the foreigner. Would he like some mead or barley beer? Here is some "tedj," which is meat stewed in barberry and mixed with fried onions and crushed pimentos. Their meal is interrupted, however. At Farré "everything belongs to Menelik," and his agent, the azage of Ankober, comes to examine the merchandise.

The next day they climb into their saddles for the last ascent. The road, barely a meter wide, winds about over precipices, then enters a forest of junipers and sycamores. The branches meet over the backs of the mules, whip the faces of the travelers, impeding their progress. Moss hangs from the trees in silvery curtains. The caravan enters a gorge carpeted with verdure and emerges finally into a natural arena of red rocks. Opposite them, on a peak, they can see groups of huts crowded within large concentric enclosures made of woven branches. This is the royal "guebi" of Ankober. After more than six weeks of exertion, fatigue, privation, Rimbaud believes he has attained his goal. It is February 6,

1887. But now comes his first great disappointment: the king is not here.

Some important events have just taken place and have changed the destiny of the country. Menelik, in an audacious campaign lasting several weeks, had taken Harrar. On the 30th of the preceding January, he had succeeded in wresting the city from the Egyptian garrison after a fierce struggle. All the Eastern mountains and the Gallas territories belong to him now: the dedjatch Waldé-Gabriel is in command of the massif of Tchertcher, the dedjatch Makonnen has just been appointed governor of Harrar by Menelik. He himself has set up his court at Antotto, the former capital of Shoa, the Addis-Ababa of the future.

This news is brought to Ankober by the explorer Jules Borelli, a native of Marseilles, who has just arrived from Antotto. His testimony with regard to Rimbaud is extremely valuable to us, as Rimbaud himself tells almost nothing about the meanderings of his expedition. Borelli notes in his journal, February 9, 1887: "Monsieur Rimbaud, a French business man, arrived to-day from Tajura with his caravan. He has been spared no troubles on the way. The usual procedure; disobedience, cupidity, and treachery on the part of his men, annoyances and ambuscades by the Adals; insufficient water, cheating by the camel-drivers. . . . Our compatriot knows Arabic and speaks the Abyssinian tongue and the dialect of the Aroussis-Gallas. He is tireless. His aptitude for languages, his great strength of will, and his patience in the face of all emergencies rank him among our most accomplished travelers."

Rimbaud's patience, however, was destined to undergo new trials. In order to see the king, Rimbaud set out for Antotto, where other difficulties awaited him.

In 1887, Menelik's court did not at all resemble the picture drawn for us, at the end of the century, by Hugues Le Roux and other European travelers. To envisage it properly at this time, one must depend rather on the descriptions of contemporaries like Rimbaud, Soleillet and Borelli: it is still a barbaric encampment, situated on the hill of Antotto. Huts cluster within enclosures of woven branches, as at Ankober. A king, ambitious and hypocritical, proverbially faithless, says Borelli, a queen mistrustful, determined, hostile to Europeans, a covetous and unsettled entourage wavering between fetichist superstition and a distorted Christianity, a few witch-doctors, one or two Coptic priests, six or seven Europeans of whom three are Swiss, an engineer, a mechanic and a carpenter, and three French traders —all these are domiciled in the royal "guebi".

Rimbaud appears before Menelik. Seated in front of his hut, clothed in a black satin chamma, the king examines the "franghi." The turban of white net knotted around his head brings out his black oily skin. Magnificent teeth, like those of a wild beast, and eager eyes blaze out of his leonine face, pitted like a colander, and his long delicate hands caress his beard with an easy gesture. Brutality and cunning, curiosity, rapacity and also intelligence show themselves in his regard. "There are my cases and guns," says Rimbaud. Menelik orders everything unpacked. He wants everything, embroidered silks and mechanical toys, parasols and trinkets, everything without discrimination. *Ego nominor leo.* His men take over the guns. But when the time comes to settle accounts, the king turns a deaf ear and goes back into his hut. Days pass, and he still refuses to come out. Finally he decides to pay only part of the charges. He claims that Labatut, Rimbaud's partner, whose obligations had been assumed by Rimbaud, had owed him money.

"My affair has turned out very badly and I feared for a while that I would come out without a cent. I found myself assaulted up there by a whole band of fake creditors of Labatut, with Menelik at their head, who robbed me of 3000 dollars (thalaris) on his account. To avoid being stripped entirely I asked Menelik to have us paid at Harrar which he had just annexed. He drew a bill for me in the Shoan manner on his oukil at Harrar, the dedjatch Makonnen."

Obviously Rimbaud did not use this last resource except in despair at doing anything better, and until he had exhausted every argument. Neither menaces nor entreaties served him. Judging from a letter from the French consul at Aden, Rimbaud's hot temper and violent passions did not help him settle his affairs. "I have been able to ascertain, sir," the consul wrote, "from the accounts that you sent me, that this operation has turned out disastrously for you, and that you did not hesitate to sacrifice your own rights to satisfy the creditors of the late M. Labatut. But I have also been made to understand from the disclosures of Europeans who have come from Shoa, and whose testimony you have called upon, that your losses would perhaps have been considerably less if, like other traders engaged in commerce with the Abyssinian authorities, you had known how to or could have complied with the peculiar exigencies of that country and of their chiefs."

Fortunately the market of Antotto was an important trading center, and Rimbaud found a few compensations there. On the plateau, a few kilometers from the "guebi," he found the Oromos squatting in lines behind their piles of skins and bags of grain. In exchange for their hides he offered them knives, mirrors, and pieces of salt crystal from Lake Assal.

Two months later he sets out for Harrar accompanied by the explorer Borelli. Thanks to Borelli's journal we are able to form an idea of this return trip about which Rimbaud has left us only meager details in a letter of August 26th to his former employer, M. Bardey.

The caravan gets under way, and leaves Ankober on May 1st, at dawn. At first they descend toward the valley of the Hawash by way of the plateau of Mindjar, passing from 3000 to 1800 meters above sea level. The road is bordered with locust, cactus and acacia, the wind is violent, the dust suffocating. Very little water is obtainable. Revictualling is difficult, their men desert them, they clash with the natives. They obtain milk, eggs, and honey in exchange for beads. They also eat wild game. At the end of a week, after crossing the "mogha," a neutral zone, or kind of no man's land lying between the tribes, where murder goes unpunished, the kalatier from Ankober refuses to go any farther. They get hold of a native by main strength and force him, at the point of a pistol, to act as guide. The caravan continues the descent slowly under a leaden sun. As soon as they perceive a crevice anywhere, half-filled with water, the men throw themselves upon it, wallow in it voluptuously, and only the curl of a whip about their bare legs can force them to get up and water the harassed mules. The country they are passing through is volcanic in character, with laval rocks and hot springs.

"We are in a Bedouin country," writes Rimbaud, "in Konollu or warm land. Brushwood and mimosa forests, inhabited by elephants and other wild animals. The Hawash has cut a deep gorge here. The whole region, on both sides of the Hawash, for two and a half days of travel, is called Careyou; the Bedouin Gallas tribes, owners of camels and other cattle, are always at war with the Aroussis. Altitude of the ford of the Hawash: about 800 meters, three feet of water. Beyond the Hawash, 30 kilometers of brush. We pass through trails made by elephants. We climb to the Itou through shaded paths. Lovely

228

wooded country, little cultivated. We return rapidly to an altitude of 2000 meters."

Borelli's account is more detailed and more interesting. He tells now of a herd of buffaloes that pass like a waterspout, now of "four hideous hippopotamus heads" emerging from the river. One feels with emotion throughout the pages of the journal the formidable mystery of the encampment at night. Ah! those nights of torpor, now weighted with silence and now full of muffled sounds, nights passed near stagnant ponds heavy with the stench of wild beasts, nights lit up by great fires built to frighten away the hyenas that haunt the shadows of the tents! The camel-drivers and muleteers lie down beside their animals. The pack-saddles are heaped one upon the other. The bridle-reins hang from the branches of the trees, among the guns stacked below against the trunks. On the ground lie empty barley sacks, skins of animals killed for food still drying in the midst of buzzing flies. One can hear the crackling of bushes at the edge of the forest under the tread of elephants. Hyenas prowl stealthily about the mules.

On the fifteenth day the caravan, emerging from the massif of Mount Ito, climbs the lower ridges of the Tchertcher. "Magnificent forest," writes Rimbaud. "A lake called Arro. We proceed along the crest of a chain of hills. The Arussi chain is on our right, paralleling our road, higher than the Ito; its immense forests and its lovely mountains are laid out in a panoramic sweep. We stop at a place

229

called Wotcho." Here there are impenetrable thickets. The lianas intertwine and hang their garlands on the branches of olive and mulberry trees. Rank vegetation swarms everywhere, there are paths encumbered with eglantine and jasmine; intoxicating perfumes mingle with the sharper smells of aromatic oils and resins, all intensified by the daily thunderstorm. As in the virgin forests of Java, Rimbaud finds here the monstrous tropical flora that adorned his adolescent dreams:

> Les fleurs pareilles à des mufles
> D'où bavent des pommades d'or
> Sur les cheveux sombres des buffles . . .
> Les calices pleins d'oeufs de feu
> Qui cuisent parmi les essences. . . .

> Flowers like animal snouts,
> From which a golden pommade
> Foams o'er the dark manes of bisons . . .
> The chalices full of fiery eggs
> Cooking in oils. . . .

Yet here he does not even look at them, as the shoe of his little Abyssinian horse treads them underfoot. It is exactly as he had predicted sixteen years before in *Ce qu'on dit au poète à propos de fleurs*. The unknown was what he desired; he spurned the realization.

On the twentieth day of the expedition, the caravan arrives at Chalanko. Skeletons lie scattered over the ground. They ride over human bones. A muleteer brings a skull and a rusty dagger to the leader.

It was here that Menelik, four months before, had cut to pieces the Egyptian garrison of Harrar. Close by the battlefield, also of tragic memory, a tree is pointed out to them as the one under which the French trader Lucereau was assassinated by the natives in 1881. But Rimbaud is not disturbed: he is now in country he knows well, and he hurries on his way, curious to see Harrar and its markets after three years of absence. May 21st, 1887, preceding Borelli by one stage, he passes through its walls of yellow stone under a deluge of rain.

And so ended this journey, more profitable in scientific results than in gold. Two conclusions were to be drawn therefrom: first, the route he used in going from the coast to Antotto, across the high desert, was dangerous and quite impractical; the exploitation of the salt deposits of Lake Assal, planned by certain French traders, seemed hardly remunerative and very difficult; caravans were exposed to attack and plundering by the Danakils. Second, the return journey—from Antotto to Harrar—over a route initiated by Rimbaud and Borelli, across pasture-land and forest, inhabited by a less savage population and with a few resources of its own, offered far less difficulty. Thus the important path of penetration into Abyssinia is determined henceforth: it goes from the coast of Somaliland by way of Harrar to Menelik's capital. The first Ethiopian railway will later follow this route.

231

☆ VII ☆

THE FACTORY AT HARRAR

WHEN Rimbaud came back to Harrar in May, 1887, he found the city considerably altered. With the Abyssinian occupation, the missionaries had come back and tried to reëstablish their influence. The dedjatch—later the notorious ras, Makonnen—had taken over and occupied the salamlik and the harem constructed in former times by the Egyptians.

Makonnen offered striking contrast to his master Menelik. He had a delicate profile, with large, enigmatic eyes, lit up as if by an internal flame, a tormented face, a thin, almost ascetic body. With forehead bound in a white head-band, and body clad in a burnous of black silk, he had rather the air of a priest or a philosopher than of a warrior. Nevertheless it was he who had organized the victory.

Harrar was a lucrative conquest for Menelik. Cotton, coffee, gum, perfumes, ivory and gold were brought there from Somaliland and Ogaden, and commerce, arrested by the war, flourished again without restraint in peace times. According to Rimbaud's realistic expression, "there was something doing there now."

Unfortunately, at that time, the city wallowed in the most frightful filth. Four thousand soldiers and two thousand slaves lived there amid the evacuations, the carcasses and the refuse of the beef on which they had been feasting. The filth of Menelik's troops had seemed less nauseating and less offensive on the windy heights of Ankober. Here, within this walled city, a fetid decay was rampant everywhere.

Rimbaud, disgusted, exhausted by the fatigues of his expedition, at end of his strength, at first sought only repose. He went to the coast, got on board ship, and went to spend a few weeks at Cairo. "My hair is quite gray," he writes from there on August 23rd, "I believe sometimes that my life hangs by a thread. Try to imagine how a man must feel after having gone through the following experiences: journeys by sea in sail-boats and journeys by land on horseback, without clothes, without provisions, without water, etc. I am excessively tired. I am bored to death. I have nothing to do at present. I fear that I may lose the little money I have. Just consider: I always carry over 40,000 gold francs about with me in my belt. They weigh about forty pounds and I am beginning to get dysentery from the load. However, I cannot return to Europe for very good reasons. In the first place I should die in the wintertime; then, I am too used to a wandering life, unrestrained and costing me nothing; finally, I have no position. Consequently I must spend the rest of

233

my days wandering under conditions of enormous
fatigue and privation with the sole prospect of dying
alone for all my pains. I shall not remain long
in these parts; I have nothing to do here. I am
forced to return to the Sudan, to Abyssinia or Ara-
bia. Perhaps I shall go to Zanzibar, from which long
journeys over Africa can be made, perhaps to China
or Japan—who knows where?"

But soon, in this eternally fermenting mind, a
definite idea arises: "to set out with one hundred
armed men and two hundred camels from Harrar
to Ambado (on the coast), the men and camels to
be supplied him for nothing by the dedjatch. At the
same time have 8000 Remingtons (without car-
tridges; the king does not need cartridges; he found
3 million of them at Harrar) delivered by boat to
the port and transferred immediately to Harrar on
the camels. As a gift to the king, a machine to
melt down the cartridges, metal plates, chemical
products and material to manufacture caps for
guns." Our anti-militarist of 1870 is certainly not
backward! He tries to obtain permission from the
French government to unload a whole arsenal at
Obok, and has his mother interest a deputy from
the Ardennes, M. Fagot, in his projects, but in vain.
The Minister of Marine, who was at that time Felix
Faure, feared difficulties with England, and, after
having alternately granted and refused authoriza-
tion, finally advised him to delay his project until
further orders . . . or counter-orders.

In the meantime—what an astonishing and para-
234

doxical decision!—Rimbaud begins writing again. Oh, not poetry, certainly. "I have written," he confides to his mother on December 15th, "an account of my journey for the *Société de Géographie*. I have sent some articles also to the *Temps*, the *Figaro*, etc. I intend to send a few interesting articles to the *Courrier des Ardennes* concerning my travels in Eastern Africa." Are we dreaming? The *Temps*, the *Figaro*, what strange literary asylums for a renegade from society and poetry! But what can we say about the *Courrier des Ardennes*, the little right-thinking newspaper of Madame Rimbaud? Shall we recall how he abused it, eighteen years before, in a letter of August 25th, 1870, cited above? Pouillard's newspaper! To be reduced to reading it, he used to say, "is a nice business . . . It is like being exiled in one's own country!" And now he is willing to contribute to the little provincial sheet so scorned formerly? Has he forgotten everything? Apparently he has. One might believe sometimes that he is waking from a long sleep. He passes his hand over his eyes. Is he dreaming? What enchanted and tragic adventure, what magic moment glimpsed, whirls up and escapes from the depths of his memory? No, no, he does not remember any more. He is a man like any other, a colonist, a planter, a merchant who has had a chance to explore a corner of the Universe . . . and that is all. Should he send a "few interesting articles to the *Courrier des Ardennes*"?

He ventures even so far as to propose to the

Temps that he enter their service as war correspondent, following the operations of the Italo-Abyssinian campaign; he is ready to leave for Massua. But his demands were probably considered too onerous, and, to console him for the refusal of the editorial board, their colonial editor, Paul Bourde, the former schoolmate to whom Rimbaud had addressed himself, informed him of his growing fame and the tardy rising of his star in the Parisian firmament.

"You probably do not know, living so far away as you do, that you have become a sort of legendary personage in a very small circle here in Paris, one of those personages who have been declared to be dead, but in whose existence a few of the faithful persistently believe and whose return is obstinately awaited. Your first efforts, in prose and verse, have been published in several magazines of the Latin Quarter, and even collected in volume form. A few young men (whom I find rather ingenuous) have tried to found a whole literary system on your sonnet about the color of the vowels. This little group, which has recognized you as master, not knowing what has become of you, hopes that you will reappear some day to raise them up out of obscurity. All this has no practical significance of any kind, I hasten to add for your complete information. But, if you will permit me to speak frankly, despite considerable incoherence and oddity, I have been struck by the astonishing virtuosity of these productions of your earliest youth. Mary (who has become a

236

very successful popular novelist) and I often speak
of you with great interest because of those produc-
tions and also because of your amazing adventures
since then."

Rimbaud scoffs at all that. His youthful verses?
Those childish things are "absurd and disgusting."
He doesn't understand how he could have done them
himself any more. What he is looking for is a re-
spectable and lucrative position, or collaboration
with some scientific enterprise. And yet all his ap-
plications are refused. Even the *Société de Gé-
ographie* refuses to give him a commission. From
then on, he has only one resource: to return to Ethi-
opia to trade and round out his little fortune. He
equips a caravan, at Zeilah, consisting of two hun-
dred camels carrying three thousand guns destined
for the dedjatch Makonnen and sets out once more
for Harrar. Here he establishes a factory in May,
1888.

At the beginning, business is "sometimes good,
sometimes bad. I am not living in the hope of be-
coming a millionaire very quickly," he writes from
Harrar, August 4, 1888; and his state of mind,
which is very low, is ingenuously revealed. "I am
very bored, always. I have never known anyone who
was capable of as much boredom as I. But isn't this
a miserable life I lead, this existence without a fam-
ily, without any intellectual occupation, lost in the
midst of negroes whose lot one would like to improve
and who try only to exploit you and make it impos-
sible for you to do your business properly. I am

237

forced to speak their gibberish, to eat their dirty
food, to bear a thousand annoyances caused by their
laziness, their treachery, their stupidity. That is
not the worst however. I am afraid of becoming
demoralized myself, isolated as I am and separated
from all intelligent society."

Fortunately the factory serves from time to time
as a local supply store for explorers. Among his
guests of passage must be mentioned the Frenchman
Borelli, the Austrian Count Teleki, and the Italian
Robecchi Brichetti. The latter recalls, in one of his
articles, evenings passed in Rimbaud's home, the
modest dinners served by candle-light by the faithful
Djami. There all languages were spoken, host and
guests commented on the Koran, discussed meteorol-
ogy and geodetics. Rimbaud almost never laughed,
the Frenchman Savouré said, but he knew how to
amuse his guests with his raillery, his irony and his
cold eccentricities. Borelli received a "cordial re-
ception" at Rimbaud's home in September, 1888.

"I first met Rimbaud," he writes, "in Aden, and
I felt myself immediately attracted to him. His man-
ner, which some found odd, and others dismissed
as being too original, was simply the result of his in-
dependent and rather misanthropic character. It
seemed to me that Rimbaud must have had some
severe disappointments in his earlier life, and that
his character had been altered indelibly by some
great misfortune. I say this, but I know nothing
definitely; for despite long hours passed together, I
never asked him anything regarding his previous
238

life, and he never offered to tell me anything. Why
did we get along so well? On certain important mat-
ters we had diametrically opposed ideas. Our pur-
pose in traveling was very different. He traveled
for business, and I in the interest of science and to
satisfy my own curiosity. Science might well have
profited more if the rôles had been interchanged!
. . . I can still see Rimbaud at work in his shop,
performing his duties with great fairness and sim-
plicity. The natives (Rimbaud used to prefer them
to Europeans) liked to come to him because he knew
their language and they could talk together, and
besides, they were always sure to find him fair in
dealings. It was very curious to observe, however,
after he had completed a deal, how he would send
off his man, looking at him slyly, then half-laugh-
ing, and throwing me an amused glance. Obviously
he was not in this business for love of it; but his
discerning nature had made him unconsciously adopt
the best way of handling the natives. At Shoa, Rim-
baud, without giving up his character as a trader,
had forced the Abyssinian chiefs to respect him for
his uprightness and his ability."

And now the factory begins to prosper rapidly.
Sugar, rice, sandals, stockings, cotton goods, silks,
trinkets, fire-arms, anything and everything, he ex-
changes for the coffee, gum, musk, ivory and gold
which are brought to him from the South. Rimbaud
exerts himself to extend his connections through-
out the whole country. His work consists not only
of barter. He must also weigh and wrap up the

goods, nail packing cases, and send them to the coast. He spares himself no trouble and does a great deal of manual labor. And when the caravans so laboriously laden arise and set out toward the coast, then new cares, new worries begin. The camels and mules carry a fortune on their backs. Will they arrive safely at their destination? Will they escape attacks by panthers and lions on the way? Perhaps the Arab who leads the caravan is in connivance with the Somali plunderers? Rimbaud waits impatiently when news does not come.

Is it surprising that he is irritable and distrustful? We cannot make of him, as does Paterne Berrichon, an angel of gentleness and charity, a saint. There is no doubt that he has ceased to be an immoralist, and curiously enough, once free of society and its laws, he imposes an elementary code of ethics on himself, of which one perceives suggestions in his correspondence. "You can well believe that my conduct is irreproachable. . . . In everything that I have done, I have been the cheated one. . . . I am working, I should like to do something good, something useful." (November 10, 1888.) "I enjoy a certain consideration because of my humane behavior. I have never injured anybody. On the contrary I do a little good whenever I can—it is my only pleasure." (February 25, 1890.) And it is true. He once even performed the good deed of a Saint Martin, by giving his burnous to a "stupid negro" who sat shivering under a torrential rain. He was both charitable and loyal. But it is difficult to go so far

as to say, with his pious biographer, Paterne Ber-
richon, that he spread everywhere "the treasure of
his goodness," and that "the natives regarded him
as if he were a divine being." His former employer,
M. Bardey, strikes a note of greater exactness when
he writes: "His caustic and biting spirit made him
many enemies. He never knew how to get rid of that
poor, wicked, satirical mask which hid the real quali-
ties of his heart."

Although Rimbaud no longer has his genius, he
still has his familiar demon. Anger flashes in him,
unexpectedly, like a beast. Stubbornness walls him
within its thorny shell. He falls out frequently with
Bardey, with Borelli. His business discussions
quickly take on a bitter and disagreeable turn. He
writes to one of his dealers to reproach him for his
"abominable coffee," his "garbage." They take him
for a "fool," an "idiot," but they are wrong. He is
not the man to be done in by them. One day he has
an argument with Borelli, about having his house
swept out, and they exchange "highly improper lan-
guage." Then, too, he does not live like a hermit. If
one can believe the accounts told to Pierre Mille
in 1896 by certain French business men of Jibuti,
"He had succeeded in learning to speak a large num-
ber of the native dialects, by forming a kind of
harem composed of women, all of different races." In
this way, they said in their pungent colonial jargon,
he had procured for himself "a set of dictionaries
bound in hide!" As one can see, he was not yet a
model of all the Christian virtues. . . .

During the years 1888-1889, his caravans gradually abandon the English port of Zeilah and direct themselves toward the new French port, Jibuti. On the other hand his commercial relations with Shoa are arrested for a time. A conflict has arisen between the king of kings, the Negus John of Abyssinia, and his vassal Menelik. Menelik holds himself on guard, recalls the dedjatch Makonnen to Antotto, "hides all his riches from the devil," and buys guns from the Italians. The threat of war hangs over the country. But the Negus John dies in 1889 in another expedition, and Menelik becomes King of Kings without having to fire a shot. "Our Menelik," writes Rimbaud, "revolted against the frightful John, and they were preparing to bite each other's noses off when the aforementioned emperor had the brilliant idea of going first to inflict punishment on the Mahdistes, near Matama. He remained there. The devil take him! Here we are at peace."

The accession of the king of Shoa to the imperial throne was favorable to business between Abyssinia and the North. Rimbaud lengthens the itinerary of his caravans and increases his shipments of firearms. He becomes purveyor by appointment to His Majesty the Negus, and receives letters patent stamped with the imperial seal. The seal consists of a heraldic lion carrying the tiara and the cross and this inscription: "The lion of the tribe of Juda has triumphed. Menelik II, the Lord's Elect, King of Kings of Ethiopia, salutes thee."

Is fortune then beginning to smile at last on him

whom she ridiculed for so long? Rimbaud has amassed by now about 80,000 francs. He could no doubt permit himself a trip to France, even—can one believe it?—a visit to the Universal Exposition of Paris. But no—he is the prisoner of his success. "My business is in no condition to be safely left, and besides, I am absolutely alone, and if I should leave, my establishment would disappear altogether." And he adds, half-seriously, half in jest: "I shall go perhaps to the next exposition or the next. Perhaps I might be able to exhibit the products of this country, perhaps even exhibit myself!"

And so the gold accumulates. He has pursued it for ten years, like a mirage. It would be pleasant to be able to imagine Rimbaud as a kind of Jason of the ideal, to see in this quest for gold the final manifestation of his insatiable thirst for possession, of his insurmountable hunger for the absolute. Alchemist of the real after having been an Alchemist of the Word, a modern Faust eternally striving for the inaccessible, he will not cease striving except in death. After exiling himself from poetry, after escaping from society, impelled by the same Claudelian desire, he will escape from this earth. His conversion might then be considered the final period, the logical and fatal conclusion of his prodigious adventure. His eye, which could not sustain the refulgence of the Word, nor the glitter of the treasures of Golconda, would come to rest finally on the gold of chasubles and altar-sticks. Like Goethe's hero, he would say to the passing moment, for the first time in his life: "Stop! You are so lovely!"

Certainly such an interpretation would be poetic: the dramatic and logical progression would be gratified thereby; the dénouement would be grandiose and brightened by celestial gleams. But the reality, despite its divergence from this picture, is none the less poignant. The vision of his fall is more moving than his glorification. In his struggle with Destiny, Rimbaud abandoned his genius and his greatness. His positivism, cynically freed from his idealistic restrictions, rid of all titanic ambitions, resigned itself finally to mediocre conquests. In the old days he had renounced poetry, perhaps burned *Une saison en enfer*, but he is ready now to contribute to the *Courrier des Ardennes!* He no longer plans to drain the last drop of life as he drained poetry and literature, to go to the end of his dream, to attempt the final scaling of death's walls, driven by the heroic passion for the Divine. No, he wants "to acquire more money," and get married. He writes to his mother, August 10, 1890: "If I could only come home and get married next spring . . . Do you think I could find someone who would be willing to travel with me?"

But even this modest wish is to be denied gratification. Jealous, implacable, Destiny waits and watches over him.

III

DEFEATED

Les femmes soignent ces féroces infirmes
retour des pays chauds.

☆ I ☆

THE RETURN

IN February of 1891, in the midst of his prosperity, Rimbaud became conscious of a sharp persistent pain in his right knee. A rapidly growing tumor formed in the affected place. The stiffening of the joint extended to the leg and withered it. He began to lose sleep and appetite. A new struggle was beginning.

At first he resists and flies into a passion. Sickness will not down him: he resists, despises, denies it. But it is stronger than he, it lays him low, nails him to his bed, tears from him an admission of his helplessness and distress. He tries another tack, attempts to circumvent it, to shift, to escape from its clutches, carry the battle into other territory, perhaps to a more equable climate, more comforts, and more intelligent care.

He has described these pathetic battles in a letter to his sister Isabelle: "This is what I have lately decided is the cause of my sickness. The climate of Harrar is cold from November to March. I have had the habit of wearing almost no clothing. A pair of cotton trousers and a cotton shirt, that is all. Clothed this way, I would take walks of from 15 to 20 kilometers a day, and senseless rides up and down the steep mountains of the country. I believe that I must have developed a form of gout in my knee out of fatigue and the alternate heat and cold. As a matter of fact the pain began as a kind of hammer-stroke on the knee-pan, a light blow every minute, attended by considerable dryness of the joint and tension of the nerve of the thigh. Then came the swelling of the veins all around the knee, which made me think it might be varicose veins. I walked about and continued to work a good deal more than before, believing that it was a simple cold. Then the pain inside the knee increased. Every step made me feel as if a nail were being driven into the side of the knee. I continued to walk about, although with increasing pain, above all I would ride on horseback, getting off the horse each time almost crippled. Then the upper part of the knee began to swell, the knee-pan stuck, the tendons were also affected. The circulation of the blood became painful and the pain spread from the ankle to the hips. I could walk only by limping very noticeably. Every day I felt worse. But I had a great deal to do, of necessity. So I began to bandage my leg from top to bottom, to massage it, bathe it, etc., without any result. Then my appetite left me. A stubborn insomnia set in. I became very weak and very thin. Toward March 15, 1891, I decided to go to bed, at least to stay on my back. I had my bed placed between my cash-box, my ac-

counts, and a window from which I could supervise
my scales at the end of the courtyard. I had to em-
ploy someone else to keep the work going while I
remained stretched out, or at least with my bad leg
stretched out. But day by day the swelling of the
knee made it look more and more like a ball. I no-
ticed that the inner side of the tibia was much larger
than on the other leg. The knee-pan became immov-
able within the suppuration from the swelling, which
in a few days, to my terror, became as hard as bone.
At this time the whole leg became stiff, completely
stiff within a week; I could not even go to the water-
closet except by dragging myself along. However,
the leg and the upper part of the thigh became
thinner, while the knee continued to swell, becoming
petrified, or rather ossified. Physically and morally
I became much weaker. At the end of March I de-
cided to leave."

It cost him considerable sacrifice to leave the low
white house surrounded by coffee trees, the terrace
where he used to rest of evenings, watching the
Southern Cross and the procession of unknown stars.
But it was even harder for him to abandon the fac-
tory, liquidate his business in the shortest possible
time, get rid of a great deal of merchandise pain-
fully acquired, at a very low price, separate him-
self from the faithful Djami, his good servant, com-
panion of his good and bad fortune. To be sure, he
had suffered in this hardly civilized country that
he had so often cursed in his moments of discourage-
ment and impatience. But at heart he was proud of

249

what he had accomplished, and when he was alone in the back of his shop, near his account-books, his glance would often fall caressingly and with pride on the bag of gold that swelled so gently in the shadow. How happy he would have been to bring back that fortune in his own good time, perhaps even increased by later efforts, to live at last in the peace of a prosperous and happy home!

He said good-by to his house, to his past, with a stricken heart. A litter covered with a leather curtain was made and he traveled in it to the coast carried by sixteen natives. It was a terrible journey. "The second day, having advanced a great distance ahead of the caravan, I was overtaken in a deserted place by a rainstorm, under which I remained stretched out for sixteen hours, without any shelter and without being able to move: it was terribly painful. On the way I could never get up from the litter. They stretched the tent above my head at the very spot where they put me down. I had to hollow out a hole in the sand with my hands near the edge of the litter, and with great difficulty I would work over on my side to ease myself. The hole I would afterwards cover over with sand."

From a page of notes scribbled from day to day, from the 7th to the 11th of April, 1891, it is easy to complete the account of the journey. The descent from the high plateaus was frightful. The bearers slid, the badly joined litter began to loosen up and threatened to capsize. Rimbaud suffered with every jolt. He tried one day to ride on a mule, with his bad leg stretched out horizontally and bound to the beast's neck, but his pain became intolerable and he had to take to his litter again. A furious wind came up, presaging a storm, and soon the sky covered over with great clouds which burst suddenly, spilling torrents of water on the whirling sands below. The storm passed over the desert in a long howl. In the confusion the caravan split up and the parts separated. The camels remained behind with the food supplies and the sick man went without anything to eat for thirty hours. Add to this the ordinary difficulties of the journey, and arguments with discontented and exhausted bearers. One day the bearers let the litter fall to the ground so brutally that Rimbaud nearly fainted with the pain. He became angry, reprimanded them for their awkwardness and impatience, and punished them by holding back part of their wages. Often, in this supreme struggle with the forces of nature and man, he lost courage and despaired of ever arriving at his journey's end.

This horrible progress through the storm, this retreat of the defeated man across the desert contrasts strikingly with the serene and funereal march, the sadly triumphal departure of the "Saint" and the "Martyr," described by Paterne Berrichon, "in the midst of the protestations and the genuflections of the weeping hordes moved by his splendid virtue." After traveling 300 kilometers in this fashion, Rimbaud arrived at Zeilah, "broken, paralyzed." He rested there hardly four hours, as a steamer was leaving for Aden immediately.

They hoisted him in his litter onto the deck, and after three days of fasting and suffering, trembling with fever and half dead with thirst, he arrived at Aden and was received at the city hospital. "I have become a skeleton," he wrote at that time. "I am frightful to behold. The bed has rubbed all the skin off my back. I don't sleep even for a moment." On May 9th, on the advice of the English doctor at Aden who admitted his inability to help him, Rimbaud made up his mind to leave, and had himself carried on board one of the ships of the *Messageries Maritimes.*

The laval rocks of the coast soon disappeared in a steaming mist. Massua, Suakim, Jidda, the Red Sea ports where he had looked for work ten years before; Alexandria, the cosmopolitan, motley-colored city from which he had set out long ago toward Cyprus and its quarries, and then the radiant Mediterranean, softly cloven by the stem of the boat and bathed in the gentleness of spring—his whole past rode in the silvery wake, a melancholy and fugitive escort. So all his efforts and misery had been useless; he was returning a poor invalid stretched out on a mattress, victim of an implacable disease and a dull despair. The setting sun, skimming the violet surface of the waters, as it came to light up his porthole, seemed to be making a derisive gesture, fortune's ironical farewell. It was with mingled feelings of relief and distress that he saw the ship enter the port of Marseilles, after "thirteen days of pain."

As soon as he debarked, however, he was "overcome by the cold," and, as he felt too weak to undertake the journey to the Ardennes, he had to enter the Hôpital de la Conception. His condition was very serious, and the doctors who examined him diagnosed it as a cancer of the bone. In order to limit the progress of the disease—while hiding their real diagnosis from him—the doctors decided to amputate his leg. This was radical treatment. But there was no time for debate. He had to submit, to resign himself. The family was informed, and Mme. Rimbaud came down from Roche.

What was this meeting like? Twelve years of silence and separation stood between her and this son that she had last seen full of strength and youth and whom she now found lying mutilated on a hospital bed. Ah, if he had only listened to her, all this would not have happened. She could not keep from complaining, from striking the moralistic note. Well, he had made a little money all the same. They began to talk business very soon. Exactly what had he brought back from that miserable country? And that draft for 36,000 francs on the Comptoir d'Escompte about which he had written her? If he had any business to be transacted at the bank, let him take advantage of her short stay in Marseilles, for she could not remain long. As a matter of fact, Isabelle was not very well, and they needed all the help they could get at Roche. They were about to begin mowing, and someone had to be watching things at the farm. A few days later, despite Rimbaud's great anger, his mother went back to the Ardennes. "As for me, I can only weep night and day. I am a dead man, I am crippled for the rest of my life. . . . And so our life is misery, misery without end! Why do we exist?"

A new ordeal awaited him. He had lived for years in fear of not being in order with the military authorities, haunted by the obsession of being arrested. And now he had hardly got off the boat when he learned that the recruiting officers were looking for him. "What new horror is this," he wrote to Roche on June 24th. "What is this tale of military service you are telling me? Ever since I was twenty-six years old, have I not been sending you a certificate proving that I was employed by a French firm in the colonies, which constitutes an exemption? And later, when I asked mamma, she answered that everything had been arranged, that I had nothing to fear." And he adds: "Prison, after what I have just gone through? Death would be better."

He lives in terror of being discovered. "I fear traps are being laid for me. I am afraid that they may get hold of my address at your post-office. . . . Do not betray me." The letters his sister sends him must be mailed from a neighboring post-office; the inscription must not mention his first name. At all costs his pursuers must be thrown off the track.

But this persecution is only imaginary. Isabelle inquires discreetly, and finds that the news is without foundation. He is not being sought for desertion, but may renew the suspension of his service until he returns to France permanently. At that time, since he is mutilated, he can simply ask to be invalided.

At the beginning of July, he tries to walk with a wooden leg, "very light, varnished, and cork-filled, very well-made (price: 50 francs)," but he only succeeds in inflaming his stump, which is still sore, and so he is forced to hobble around his room on crutches. Who would not be moved by the pathetic lamentations that arise from his letters at this time: "What annoyance! What weariness! How sad, too, to think of all my old travels, and how active I was only five months ago! Where is my mountain-climbing, horseback-riding, long walks, deserts, rivers, seas? And now I lead the life of a cripple! I who had just decided to return to France this summer to get married! Good-by marriage! Good-by family, good-by future! My life is finished! I am simply a motionless stump now!"

As one can see, he is neither resigned nor stoical; he is desperate. He is a defeated man who weeps over his defeat. Where is the daring horseman of the high Ethiopian plateaus? "Your head and shoulders stick out in front and you swell behind like a hump-back. People grin to see you skipping about. When you sit down again, your hands are trembling, your arm-pits raw, your face idiotic." Could one have imagined a more tragic destiny, more bitter tears? He had been so quiveringly unstable, so prodigiously mobile, he had had such

255

a furious passion for change, so much spirit, such ardor, such life, and now all this was petrified as if by some frightful sorcery! One would say that death had already touched him with an icy finger; he is caught in the leaden snare. The rigidity spreads to the other limbs. This living body stiffens in a death-like ossification. The other leg, the shoulder, the arm, are attacked little by little. "Can I have some disease of the bones?" the miserable man asks himself.

Then he makes a supreme effort. His whole being strains itself to make one gesture of savage energy, one last heroic revolt against fate. He has himself carried to the railroad station, and lifted into a train. Where is he going? To the farm of his childhood, to reëstablish contact with the soil.

Here is the little station at Vonq and the canal bordered with sad poplars. The railroad employees let him down from the train carefully and install him in the waiting room, as the carriage from Roche has not arrived. Night falls. A cool mist envelopes the trees, dwarfs the outlines of things. Finally he hears the jingling of bells on the road and the trot of the old mare Comtesse. Isabelle leaps into his arms. They look at each other. How they have both changed! She was thirteen when he went away and now she is a woman. And he? Ah, he is but a ghost!

"The first day," she writes, "as he entered his room, the finest in the house and prepared for him with naïve care, he made the sincere and flattering exclamation: 'This is just like Versailles.' We had

256

opened his trunks right away, arranged his things around the room, foreseen and prepared for all the needs of an invalid and a weary traveler." But Rimbaud is cold, he shivers in this old damp house that a mean, gray summer does not succeed in warming up. What a sad year! A frost kills the wheat. Two weeks after his return, a terrific storm bursts during the night, and hail devastates the gardens. The next day a late frost completes the work of stripping the trees. Then comes persistent rain, gray, monotonous, soaking everything, discouraging and chilling the soul. The ruined harvest rots beneath the lowering sky, all hope dies. However, Rimbaud has a reaction, tries to grip himself again. "As he found it extremely distasteful to remain quietly at home, he went out a great deal in an open carriage. Every day, despite his fatigue and the bad weather, he would spend the afternoon driving. He loved to be taken to places where he could see a gay crowd, on Sundays and holidays; and, without mixing with them at all, he would enjoy watching the movements and the gestures of the people, as well as the changes in customs that ten years had made."

But the malady began to gain ground: the severed thigh-bone increased in size and his arm became rigid. As the jolting of the carriage tortured him, he had to remain at home, but even there an unbearable pain in the arm-pit prevented him from going about on crutches and kept him motionless in his arm-chair. The nights were especially frightful. He was tormented by insomnia, his mind emptied of all

257

thought. Then he began to take narcotics, drank poppy-seed tea and lived for several days in a strange dream. He had the shutters closed, the lamps lit, and began to play the hand-organ, living over his life aloud. "His voice, gentle, somewhat slow," writes Isabelle, "took on an accent of penetrating beauty; oriental turns of expression and phrases borrowed from other European languages were interspersed in his speech." After a few days of intoxication, he became prey to hallucinations. "One night, imagining himself whole again and trying to seize some apparition now here, now there, hiding perhaps in some corner of the room, he tried to get off his bed alone and pursue the illusory creature. We all ran to him at the sound of his heavy fall; his long body was stretched out quite naked on the carpet." The shock sobered him. He ceased taking those palliatives that bereft him of his reason, he renounced those insidious dreams that disarmed his soul and lowered the walls of silence with which it was surrounded. . . .

* * *

"No, no, enough. I must go away!" Roche—"land of wolves"—now horrifies him. Sunlight! Warmth! Ah, who will rescue him from the gloomy Ardennes? Harrar, Harrar, where art thou? Thy tawny scorched arena whirls in the sunlight around the white mosque whose shadow is blue on the main square. Go, go, at least as far as Marseilles, and watch the departure of the steamers! . . . One month after his arrival at Roche, Sunday, August 23, 1891, accompanied by Isabelle, he makes his last voyage toward the South.

It was a Calvary. In the first place, although he had risen before dawn, he missed the morning train. Moaning, he returned to the farm once again, shivering in the cold mist that bit into his bones and filmed the jolting carriage with moisture. At about ten o'clock, as he was about to set off again for the station, his heart failed him. "Stay, will you? We shall take good care of you." No, fate has decided otherwise. Let's go! The servants put him into the carriage—this time he leaves two hours ahead of time. A weary wait at the station at Vonq. Noon comes at last. The train carries him away. The martyrdom begins. The shaking of the railway carriage torments him, shooting pains dart all over his body, the torture is so great that he cries out. He collapses on the cushions, holding his stump in his two hands: "It hurts! It hurts!" The infernal journey protracts itself interminably. The window frames the chalky Champagne countryside and the green Ile-de-France. A pair of newly-weds enter the compartment. The suburbs of Paris unfold under a fugitive ray of sunlight. Rimbaud dozes. The whole world is held under the Sunday spell. The villas have a holiday air decked with blooming dahlias; life seems to bestow a last ironic smile on her wounded victim. But here is the Gare de l'Est. Evening has come. The train is emptied. Should he remain here a while, in this Paris that he left eighteen

259

years ago, and where, without his knowledge, his glory and his legend are growing apace? The rain begins to fall, the cab slides over the wet streets. No, to the Gare de Lyon! His face glued to the pane, examining the city where his past life stirs mysteriously, he flees into the shadows.

He leaves for Marseilles on the eleven o'clock express. He passes a night of delirium, a day of torpor and hallucination. After thirty hours of traveling, he gets off at Saint-Charles and comes back to the Hôpital de la Conception, where he registers as *Jean* Rimbaud.

They give him a little room shaded by a stone gallery and thick plane trees outside. The autumn light filters in through leaves that turn golden before they die. Moving shadows prowl around the walls. There is a silence as of the tomb. The sunlight fades.

☆ II ☆

CONVERSION AND DEATH

THE fixed idea of returning to Harrar still haunted the sick man. He continued to hope that a miracle would happen to make him well and permit him to set out for the East. The doctors humored him, but his sister was informed of the truth. One month after their arrival, September 22, 1891, she wrote to her mother, whose persistent silence worried her: "There is no hope for his recovery. His disease must be the same cancer spreading through the bone-marrow which necessitated the amputation of his leg." She watched over him with extraordinary patience. In *Une saison en enfer* he had himself predicted, "The women nurse these fierce invalids returned from lands of burning heat." Despite its tardy flowering, this outburst of fraternal love is very touching, as Isabelle clasps the intractable invalid in a desperate and fervent embrace. "No hands but mine have nursed him, have touched him, dressed him, helped him in his suffering. No mother has ever felt a greater concern for her sick child than I." She alone did not abandon him.

While he was dying in Marseilles, Mme. Rimbaud maintained a sulky silence at Roche. She bore Isabelle a grudge because her daughter had refused the offer of a wealthy marriage—"a good match." She was annoyed too, though she dared not say so, that Isabelle had left her alone on the farm, at harvest time, to cater to the last whims of a dying brother who had long been lost to his family. On the pressing demand of Isabelle who entreated her "on her knees" to write, this is what she answered: Her daughter was "very unreasonable." It was she who deserved sympathy, with servants eating her out of house and home, with drunken farmhands, and the old mare Comtesse sick into the bargain! If she could only get some assistance! Couldn't Isabelle leave Arthur, if only for a fortnight? Harsh and egotistic, the terrible woman reverses the rôles to such an extent that her daughter takes pity on her. "Have patience and be firm with the servants. Father Warin or someone else can thresh the little wheat we have for forage. . . ." Isabelle forgets her invalid for a moment to sympathize with her mother for having so much to do, to inquire about the work on the farm, about the little Breton cow that "will calve at the beginning of November," about the pigs that "ought to be good and fat enough for market." But she is uneasy as she writes. Was that not a groan she heard? She interrupts her letter for a moment to approach the bedside. No, he is still, he sleeps "with his eyes open," his breath coming in gasps, and so thin and pale with his eyes sunken and great rings about them. "I must not think of leaving Arthur," she continues in her letter, "he is very sick, he is weaker every day. . . . I ask only one thing now—that he may die within the church!"

That is her dearest wish: that he be converted! He has no resignation and the gentle virtues of grace do not descend upon him. He does not *want* to die. Whenever he is awake, he weeps, swears, blasphemes. There is nothing more heart-rending, more pathetic to her than his sacrilegious distress.

How could anyone have made a Christian out of him, even a Christian unknown to himself? His adolescence was one long cry of impiety, his *Saison en enfer* was, as someone has said, "a rejection of God," his letters from Abyssinia, ranging over more than ten years, do not show the slightest spiritual relenting. His atheism, to be sure, is not strikingly apparent either, but his thought processes are always strangely irreligious or indifferent to religion, and at the least agnostic. To his mother, who was so orthodox and so bigoted, he wrote, "We live and die by another pattern than we could ever have designed, and that without hope of any kind of compensation. We are lucky that this is the only life we shall have to lead, and that that is obvious, etc." This is the man whose supposed conversion has been dated back as far as 1873, after the drama of Brussels. We need only see him on his death-bed to be convinced that he is still far from God, and to understand the Christian pangs of his sister.

He shows no patience, no submission. "He threatens to strangle himself or commit suicide by any means if I leave him." As an invalid he is insufferable. "He cannot bear a wrinkle in the sheet under him." "When his meal is brought to him, he finds fault with everything and touches almost nothing." "I arrange his bed, his blankets, his pillows continually; he is never comfortable. He never stops complaining for an instant." Whatever his sufferings may be, is this really the state of mind of a dying Christian? His mind is the prey of countless irritable whims. "I am at my wits' end all day long to prevent him from committing countless follies." In his delirium he is the victim of evil spirits: "He accuses the nurses and even the sisters of abominable things which cannot possibly be true; I tell him that he has probably dreamed them, but he will not confess his error and tells me that I am a simpleton and an idiot."

However death is approaching quickly now. An electric treatment proves to be as useless as it is painful. Rimbaud spends his days weeping. "I shall go into the earth," he says to Isabelle, "and you will walk in the sun." It is time to reconcile him to God. Isabelle thinks only of this and busies herself in preparing him for it. Her faith and her tenderness give her courage, resolution. Marvelous exaltation! Her love for God and for her brother unite in an exaltation of religious passion. She urges the chaplains to come and see Rimbaud.

He receives them twice, but "with so much lassitude and discouragement" that they dare not speak to him of the last sacraments. At Isabelle's request, all the nuns of the hospital offer up prayers, one Saturday evening, "that he may die within the church." Divine mercy cannot resist such appeals, such desperate entreaties. The following Wednesday, October 28th, Isabelle, elated, announces to her mother the miraculous and poignant news. "God be praised a thousand times! On Sunday I experienced the greatest happiness I can have in this world. It is no longer a poor reprobate who is dying beside me; it is an upright soul, a saint, a martyr, one of the elect. . . . Sunday morning, after high mass, he seemed calmer, and in full possession of his faculties. One of the chaplains came to him and offered to confess him; and he consented. . . . When I came back to him, Arthur was very moved, but he did not weep; he was sad but serene, as I had never beheld him. He looked into my eyes as he had never looked before. He asked me to come very close to him, then said: "You are of the same blood as I. Do you believe, tell me, do you believe?" I answered: "I do believe, others wiser than I have believed and do believe. And then I am sure at present, that is to say, I have the proof!' He said then bitterly, 'Oh, yes, they say that they believe, they pretend to be converted, but that is only to get people to read what they have written. It's just a kind of speculation.' I hesitated a moment, then I said, 'Oh no, they would make much more money out of blasphemy!' He continued to look at me with heaven in his eyes. I returned his regard. He wanted to embrace me, then: 'It is really possible that we have the same soul, since we are of the same blood. You believe then?' I repeated: 'Yes, I believe, we must believe.' Then he said, 'You must prepare everything in the room, put everything in order; he is going to return with the sacraments. You shall see, they will bring candles and altar cloths, you must put white linen everywhere. I am, then, very sick.' . . . Since then he blasphemes no more, he calls to Christ on the Cross and he prays! Yes, he prays!"

And so the miracle is accomplished. Grace has been vouchsafed like a sudden illumination to the miserable man. Who would have thought it possible? "Yes, he prays, he!" He who had only abuse and defiance on his lips! The rebel has submitted, the damned soul has become the elect! But the battle with the forces of the devil was hard fought, the issue not always certain. As he left the room, the priest confided to the trembling Isabelle in a mysterious voice: "Your brother has faith, my child, what were you telling us before? He has faith, and I have never beheld such faith."

It is true, in Rimbaud the old devouring instinct has been reawakened: his ungovernable thirst for moral infinitude, for perfection, is reaffirmed. His hunger for the absolute slumbering in the depths of his consciousness has thrown itself for sustenance upon the hopes offered by Catholicism. But as soon as he is alone with his sister, his faith wavers; he hesitates, fumbles, seeks support from her. "Do you believe? Tell me, do you believe? . . . You believe, then?"

In the days following, life detaches itself from him; his soul leaves the inert mass that his body has become. Between these two, there is no longer anything in common. A mass of petrified flesh is there upon the bed, consumed by an enormous cancer, a tumor on the thigh that swells, a monstrous excrescence, between the hip and the abdomen—a skeleton-like trunk surrounded by limbs already dead. Morphine drugs this body as it dries, hardens, cracks everywhere, dissolves. From now on a distant voice arises as from the depths of a dream. The thought of the dying man is breathed forth in obscure and musical confidences. Are they final illusions or supreme lucidity? Paul Claudel has sought in these last manifestations proof that his genius had not been extinguished, but was merely chained, or mute, and that in breaking the fetters of his long silence it regained its liberty, its superhuman flight into death.

"Though awake," writes Isabelle, "he completes his life in a kind of continual dream. He says strange things very gently, in a voice that would be enchanting if it were not heartrending. He speaks his dreams—however, it is not at all the same as when he was delirious. One would think—and I believe it —that he does it on purpose. . . . He blends everything . . . artfully." Is it possible? Who can penetrate the mystery of this melodious lethargy through which pass images of Ethiopian caravans and the shadow of the faithful Djami? "Allah Kerim," he cries, "Allah Kerim!" The exotic dream seems to revive and dominate, with its rich and colorful tones, the Christian aspiration. In these visions of an unattainable Islam, one detects more Oriental lyricism than Catholic effusion. But who would dare draw any definite conclusion? Did the prodigious author of the *Illuminations*, the Symbolist of *Une saison en enfer*, in one final transposition, say farewell to earth and salute the Elysian dawn? Above this corpse, in the half-light of his death agony, at the indefinable limits of light and shadow, there blossoms a strange flower that I fear to violate.

On November 9th, Arthur Rimbaud dictated a brief and incoherent letter, probably to the manager of a steamship company: "Tell me at what hour I can be carried on board?"

The next day death came and led him on board the funeral boat.

He was thirty-seven years old.

*　　　*　　　*

A few days later, the coffin of the poet arrived at the railroad station in Charleville. His mother went to find Abbé Gillet, curé of the parish church, at eight o'clock in the morning, and ordered a first-class service for ten o'clock. "But, madame, that is very short notice. You can't get a thing like that up in a jiffy." The curé added that he had formerly been the boy's religious instructor and that

he would like to invite some of his former school-
mates to the obsequies. But in her driest voice she
cut him short: "Do not insist, Monsieur le curé, it
is useless!"

The interment took place at the hour arranged,
with the conventional ceremony. Passers-by in the
street stopped to examine the strange cortège: who
could this dead man be, so abandoned by the living?
Two persons followed the hearse, two women in
black, silent: the mother and the sister.

*　　*　　*

He sleeps beside them calmly in the Charleville
cemetery, in the family tomb, surrounded by a mod-
est railing and decorated by a white rose-bush.

Opposite the railroad-station, "on the square di-
vided up into mean little lawns," in the midst of
the din of trains, his monument, decapitated during
the invasion [1] raises its shaft without a bust, like
a broken lyre.

[1] The Germans during the war confiscated the bronze bust of
the poet, and the Municipal Council of Charleville has recently
decided to restore the monument.

APPENDIX

A SEASON IN HELL

Once on a time, if I remember rightly, my life was a feast where all hearts opened and every wine ran.

One evening I set Beauty on my knees.—And I found her sour.—And I cursed her.

I took arms against justice.

I fled. O sorcerers, misery, and hatred, it is to you my treasure has been entrusted!

I was able to obliterate from my mind all human hope. Upon each joy, to strangle it, I made the soundless spring of a wild beast.

I called the executioners that, dying, I might bite the butts of their guns. I called the scourges to choke me with sand, with blood. Misfortune was my god. I stretched myself out in the mud. I dried myself in the air of crime. And I played folly some good tricks.

And Spring brought me the frightful laugh of an idiot.

Now, just lately, finding I was on the edge of giving my last gasp, it occurred to me to look for the key to the ancient feast, where I might perhaps find appetite again.

273

Charity is that key.—An inspiration which proves that I have been dreaming.

"You shall remain a hyena, etc. . . ." shrieks the fiend who crowned me with such amiable poppies. "Earn death with all your appetites and your egoism and all the capital offenses."

Ah! I have taken too much of it:—But, dear Satan, I beg you a less petulant eye! and while awaiting the several little misdeeds in arrears, you who admire in a writer the absence of all that might be descriptive or edifying, I detach for your benefit these few hideous pages from my damned man's diary.

BAD BLOOD

From my Gallic ancestors I get my pale blue eyes, narrow skull and awkwardness in fight. I find my costume as barbarous as theirs. Only I do not butter my hair.

The Gauls were the clumsiest beast-flayers and grass-burners of their time.

From them I get: idolatry and love of sacrilege;—Oh! all the vices, rage, sensuality—magnificent sensuality;—above all dying and laziness.

I have a horror of all trades. Masters or workmen, all peasants, low-born. The hand at the pen is no worse than the hand at the plow,—and no better. What a century for hands! I will never have my hand. After that, family life leads too far. The propriety of begging wounds me to death. Criminals are disgusting like geldings; as for me, I am intact, and don't care.

274

But! who made my tongue so deceitful that up to now it has guided and guarded my laziness? Without having earned my bread even with my body, lazier than a toad, I have lived everywhere. Not a family of Europe that I do not know.—I mean families like my own which hold everything from the declaration of the Rights of Man.—I have known every son of a family!

If I had antecedents at any point whatever in French history!

But no, nothing.

It is perfectly evident to me that I have always belonged to the under race. I cannot comprehend rebellion. My people never rose except to pillage: so wolves the animal they have not killed.

I call to mind the history of France, eldest daughter of the Church. As a *vilain* I must have made the journey to the Holy Land; I have in my head routes in the Suabian plain, views of Byzantium, of the ramparts of Solyma; the cult of Mary, the yearning over the Crucified, awake in me among a thousand profane fairy tales.—I am seated among broken pots and nettles, leprous, at the bottom of a wall gnawed by the sun.— Later, to continue, I must have bivouacked under Germany's nights.

Ah! again: I dance the sabbath in a red clearing with old women and children.

I do not remember myself farther back than this country and Christianity. I shall never finish seeing myself again in this past. But alone always, with no family: what language did I use to speak, even? I

275

never see myself at the councils of Christ; nor at the councils of the Lords,—the representatives of Christ.

What was I in the last century? I do not find myself again till today. No more migrations, no more vague wars. The under race has overrun everything—the people, as they say, reason, the nation, and science.

Oh! science! They have reclaimed it all. For the body and for the soul—the viaticum—they have medicine and philosophy—old women's remedies and popular songs rearranged. And the amusements of the princes and the games they used to forbid. Geography, cosmography, mechanics, chemistry! . . .

Science, the new nobility! Progress. The world advances! Why should it not turn?

It is the vision of numbers. We are on our way to the *Spirit*. It is quite certain, it is oracular, what I say. I understand, and as I do not know how to explain myself without pagan words, I wish to be silent.

The pagan blood returns! The Spirit is near; why does Christ not help me by giving my soul nobility and freedom? Alas, the Gospel has gone by! the Gospel! the Gospel.

I await God greedily. I belong to the under race for all eternity.

Here I am on the Breton coast. The cities light up at evening. My day's work is done; I am leaving Europe. The sea air shall burn my lungs; lost climates shall tan me. Swim, pound roots, hunt, above all smoke; drink liquor strong as boiling metal,—as those dear ancestors of mine did formerly round their fires!

I will return with limbs of iron, dark-skinned, furious-eyed; from my mask they shall think me of a strong race. I will have money: I will be indolent and brutal. Women tend these terrible invalids back from the hot countries. I will get mixed up in politics. Saved!

Now I am outcast, I have a horror of my country. The best thing would be sleep, quite drunk, on the beach.

You don't go—Reenter the old ways here, loaded down with my vice, the vice which has sent its roots of suffering into my side ever since the age of reason,—which towers to the sky, strikes me, knocks me down, drags me along.

Last innocence and last timidity. It is said. Not bring my disgusts and betrayals to the world.

Come! The march, the burden, the desert, ennui and anger.

To whom am I to hire myself out? What animal must be adored? What holy image assaulted? What hearts shall I break? What lie ought I to hold to?—In what blood walk?

Rather keep myself clear of the law.—A hard life, a plain self-stultification,—lift with withered fist the lid of the coffin, sit down, suffocate. In this way be rid of old age and dangers: fear is not French.

—Ah! I am so weary that I offer my impulses toward perfection to no matter what divine image.

O my self-abnegation, my marvelous charity! down here, however.

De profundis, Domine, am I a fool!

While still a child I used to admire the incurable malefactor upon whom the prison hulks shut forever;

277

I visited the inns and lodgings that he might have consecrated by his sojourn; I saw with his *idea* the blue sky and the flowered work of the country; I used to scent his fatality in the cities. He had more strength than a saint, more good sense than a traveller—and he, he alone! as witness of his glory and of his rightness.

On the high-roads, winter nights, shelterless, unclothed, without bread, a voice clenched my frozen heart: "Weakness or strength: you see, it is strength. You know neither where you are going nor why you go; enter everywhere, respond to all. They will not kill you any more than if you were a corpse." In the morning I had so lost a gaze, and a face so dead, that the people whom I met perhaps *did not see me*.

In the cities the mud seemed to me suddenly red and black, like a mirror when the lamp moves in the next room, like a treasure in the forest! "Good luck," I cried, and I saw a sea of flame and smoke up to heaven, and right and left all wealth blazing like a billion thunder-storms.

But debauchery and the companionship of women were forbidden me. Not even a comrade. I used to see myself before the angry crowd, confronting the cordon of executioners, weeping over their inability to understand, and forgiving them!—Like Jeanne d'Arc!— "Priests, professors, school masters, you are wrong to turn me over to justice. I have never belonged to this people; I have never been a Christian; I belong to the race that sang in punishment. I do not under-

stand, and forgiving them!—Like Jeanne d'Arc!—
beast: you are making a blunder."

Yes, my eyes are shut to your light. I am a brute,
a negro. But I can be saved. You are false negroes,
you, maniacs, savages, misers. You, merchant, are a
negro; you, magistrate, a negro; you, general, a negro;
emperor, old itch, you are a negro: you have drunk
untaxed liquor of Satan's manufacture.—This people
is inspired by fever and cancer. Invalids and old men
are so respectable that they demand boiling. The spite-
fullest thing would be to quit this continent where
madness prowls in search of hostages for these wretches.
I am going to the true kingdom of the children of Ham.

Did I still know nature? Did I know myself?—
No more words. I bury the dead in my belly. Shouts,
drum, dance, dance, dance, dance! I do not even see
the hour when the whites will disembark and I shall
fall into nothingness.

Hunger, thirst, shouts, dance, dance, dance, dance!'
The whites are landing. The cannon! You must
submit to baptism, put on clothes, work.

I have felt the finishing stroke at my heart. Ah!
I had not expected it!

I have never done evil. My days are going to be
easy, I shall be spared repentance. I shall not have
endured the tortures of the soul almost dead to virtue,
in whom the severe light comes back to life like funeral
candles. The lot of the son of the house, premature
coffin covered with limpid tears. Without doubt de-
bauchery is stupid, vice is stupid; filth must be thrown
away. But the clock will not have arrived at the point

of striking no hour but that of pure woe. Am I going to be carried off like a child to play in paradise, forgetful of all unhappiness?

Quick! are there other lives? Sleep in wealth is impossible. Wealth has always been very public. Divine love alone can provide the keys of knowledge. I see that nature is nothing but a display of goodness. Farewell, chimeras, ideals, errors!

The reasonable hymn of the angels rises from the ship of salvation: it is divine love.—Two loves! I can die of earthly love, die of devoutness. I have left souls behind whose grief will grow at my departure. You choose me from among the shipwrecked; those who remain, are they not my friends?

Save them!

Reason is born in me. The world is good. I will bless life. I will love my brothers. These are no longer childish promises. Nor the hope of escaping old age and death. God is my strength, and I praise God.

I am no longer in love with disgust. Rage, debauchery, folly—whose every impulse and disaster I know— all my burden is laid aside. Consider without reeling the extent of my innocence.

I should no longer be able to ask for the solace of a bastinado. I do not fancy myself embarked on a wedding with Jesus Christ for father-in-law.

I am not the prisoner of my reason. I have said: God. I want freedom in salvation: how am I to seek it? Frivolous inclinations have left me. No more need of devotions or of God's love. I do not regret the century of impressionable hearts. Every one to his own reason, contempt, and charity. I retain my place at the top of this angelic ladder of good sense.

As for settled happiness, domestic or not . . . no, I am incapable of it. I am too dissipated, too weak. Life blooms through work, old truism; my life is not heavy enough, it soars and floats high above action, that dear pivot of the world.

What an old maid I am becoming, to lack the courage to be in love with death!

If God granted me the heavenly, aerial quietude of prayer,—like that of the ancient saints.—The saints, strong men! The hermits, artists such as we have need of no longer!

Continual farce? My innocence would make me weep. Life is the farce to lead everywhere.

Enough! here is chastisement.—*March!*

Ah! my lungs burn, my temples roar! Night rolls through my eyes in this sunlight! Heart . . . limbs . . .

Where are we going to bathe? I am weak! the others advance. Tools, weapons . . . time . . .

Fire, fire on me! There! or I surrender.—Cowards!— I kill myself! I throw myself under the horses' hoofs!

Ah! . . .

—I shall get used to it.

This would be the French life, the path of honour!

NIGHT IN HELL

I have swallowed a famous throatful of poison.— Thrice blest be the counsel that came to me.—My bowels broil. The shock of the poison twists my limbs, distorts me, throws me to earth. I am dying of thirst, suffocating, I cannot cry out. It is hell, it is the ever-lasting torment. See how the fire blazes up! I am burn-ing properly. Away, demon!

I had caught a glimpse of my conversion to virtue and happiness, my salvation. Can I describe the vision? The atmosphere of hell is not congenial to hymns. There were millions of charming creatures, a bland concert of spirits, strength and peace, noble ambitions, I know not what else.

Noble ambitions!

And this is life still!—Suppose damnation were eternal! A man who wants to mutilate himself is quite damned, is he not? I believe that I am in hell, therefore I am. It is the catechism at work. I am the slave of my baptism. Parents, you contrived my misfortune and your own. Poor innocent!—Hell cannot touch the heathen.—This is life still. Later the delights of dam-nation will be more profound. A crime, quick, and I fall into nothingness beyond the laws of men.

Silence, there, silence! Shame, reproach here: Satan who says the fire is mean, my rage appallingly out of place.—Enough! . . . Of the errors they deplore in me, magic, false perfumes, childish tunes.—And they tell me that I hold the truth, that I perceive justice: I have a sane, well-bridled judgment, I am ready for perfection. . . . Pride.—My scalp is parched. Pity! Lord, I am afraid. I am thirsty, so thirsty. Ah! child-hood, the grass, the rain, the lake on the pebbles, *the full moon when the clock was striking twelve.* . . .

282

The devil is in the belfry at this hour. Mary! Holy Virgin! . . .—Horror at my inanity.

Out there, are those not honest souls who wish me well? . . . Help . . . I have a pillow on my mouth, they do not hear me, they are phantoms. Besides, no one ever thinks of others. Let them keep off. I smell of seared flesh, like a heretic; there is no doubt about it.

The hallucinations are innumerable. Just what I have always had; no more faith in history, forgetfulness of principles. I will keep them to myself; poets and visionaries might be jealous. We are a thousand times the richest; let us be close-fisted like the sea.

There! a moment ago the clock of life stopped. I am no longer in the world. Theology is serious, hell is certainly *down below,*—and heaven above.—Ecstasy, nightmare, sleep in a nest of flames.

What tricks of attention in the country . . . Satan, Ferdinand, runs with the wild grain . . . Jesus walks on the purple briers, without their bending. Jesus was walking on the angry waters. The lantern showed him to us standing, white with brown locks, on the flank of an emerald wave. . . .

I am going to unveil all the mysteries: mysteries of religion or of nature, death, birth, future, past, cosmogony, nonexistence. I am master of phantasmagoria.

Listen! . . .

I have all the talents!—There is nobody here, and there is somebody. I should not care to squander my treasure.—Do you want negro songs, houri dances?

283

Do you want me to vanish, to plunge after the *ring?*
Do you? I will make gold, remedies.

Trust in me, then; faith assuages, guides, cures. All,
come,—even little children, that I may console you,
that his heart may be poured out for you like water,—
the marvellous heart!—Poor human beings, toilers! I
do not ask you for prayers; with your faith alone
I shall be happy.

And think of me. This makes me barely regret the
world. I have a chance of not suffering any more. My
life consisted of mild follies only, it is to be regretted.

Bah! make all the grimaces imaginable!

Decidedly we are out of the world. No longer any
sound. The sense of touch has left me. Ah! my castle,
my Saxony, my wood of willow trees. Evenings, morn-
ings, nights, days. . . . Am I tired!

I ought to have my hell for anger, my hell for
pride,—and the hell of laziness; a concert of hells.

I am dying of lassitude. It is the grave. I am going
to the worms, horror of horrors! Satan, you clown,
you want to dissolve me with your charms. I demand.
I demand! a fork-thrust, a drop of fire.

Ah! climb back to life! Gaze at our deformities. And
this poison, this kiss a thousand times accursed! My
weakness, the cruelty of the world! My God, pity, hide
me, I am too ill!—I am hidden and I am not.

It is the fire waking again with its damned.

DELIRES I

FOOLISH VIRGIN——THE INFERNAL BRIDEGROOM

Hear the confession of a companion in Hell:

"O heavenly Bridegroom, my Lord, do not deny the confession of the most unhappy of thy servants. I am lost. I am drunken. I am unclean. What a life!

"Forgive me, heavenly Lord, forgive me! Ah! forgive me! what tears! And what tears again, later on, I trust!

"Later on I shall know the heavenly Bridegroom! I was born subject to Him.—The other can beat me now!

"At present, I am at the bottom of the world, O my friends! . . . no, not my friends. . . . Never delirium nor torture to equal these. . . . Is it ridiculous!

"Ah! I suffer, I cry out. I suffer truly. Nevertheless all is allowed me, loaded with the contempt of the most contemptible hearts.

"At any rate let me make this avowal, free to repeat it twenty other times,—as depressing, as insignificant!

"I am the slave of the infernal Bridegroom, the one who ruined the foolish virgins. It is surely that same demon. It is not a ghost, not a phantom. But I, who have lost my wisdom, who am damned and dead to the world—they will not kill me! How describe him to you! I no longer know how to talk even. I am in black, I weep, I am afraid. A little freshness, Lord, if you will, if you will well.

285

"I am a widow . . .—I used to be a widow . . .—
why yes, I was perfectly respectable at one time, and
I was not born to become a skeleton! . . . He was al-
most a child. . . . His mysterious delicacies had led me
astray. I forgot my every human duty to follow him.
What a life! Real life is absent. We are no longer in
the world. I go where he goes, it is necessary. And
often he grows furious at me, *me, poor soul*. The De-
mon!—He is a demon, you know, *he is not a man*.

"He says: 'I do not care for women: love must be
reinvented, that's understood. They can do no more
than desire a snug situation. When they have it, heart
and beauty are discarded; the only thing that is left is
cold contempt, the rations of marriage, nowadays. Or
else I see women, clearly marked for happiness, whom
I might have made into good comrades, devoured first
by brutes as tender-hearted as a pile of faggots. . . .!'

"I listen to him making shame a glory, cruelty a
charm, 'I belong to a far-off race: my ancestors were
Norsemen: they used to pierce their sides, drink their
blood. I will make gashes all over my body, I will tattoo
myself; I want to grow hideous like a Mongol: you
shall see, I will bellow through the streets. I want to
grow quite mad with rage. Never show me any jewels,
I should grovel and go into contortions on the carpet.
My wealth, I want it stained with blood all over. Never
will I work. . . .' On several nights, becoming pos-
sessed of his demon, we rolled one another about, I
fought with him!—Often at night, when he is drunk, he
lies in wait for me in the streets or in the house to
frighten me to death.—'They will actually cut off my

286

neck; it will be disgusting.' Oh! those days when he wants to walk with an air of crime!

"Sometimes he speaks in a sort of tender child's talk, of death that brings repentance, of the miserable wretches there must be, of grievous toil, of farewells that rend the heart. In the stews where we used to get drunk, he would weep as he watched the people round us, the live stock of squalor. He picked up drunkards out of the black streets. He had a bad mother's pity for little children.—He would move winsomely like a little girl at the catechism.—He would pretend to be informed about everything, business, art, medicine. I followed him, it was necessary.

"I was witness to all the adornment with which he surrounded himself in spirit; garments, cloths, furniture; I lent him weapons, a different face. I saw all that touched him, just as he would have liked to create it for himself. When his spirit seemed to me apathetic, I followed him far in strange and complicated actions, good or bad; I was certain never to enter his world. Beside his dear, sleeping body, what hours I have watched at night, seeking to learn why he was so anxious to escape from reality. Never was there a man with such a vow as that. I recognized,—without being afraid for him,—that he might be a serious danger to society. —Perhaps he possesses secrets that *will change life.* No, I replied to myself, he is only looking for them. Finally his kindness is enchanted, and I am its prisoner. No other soul would have the strength,—the strength of despair!—to endure it, to be loved and protected by him. Besides, I would not picture him to myself with

another soul: one sees his Angel, never another's Angel,
—I believe. I used to exist in his soul as in a palace
which they have made empty in order not to see so
mean a person as yourself: that was all. Alas! I was
very dependent on him. But what did he want of my
colourless and facile being? He would not improve
me, unless he were to make me die. Sadly mortified, I
sometimes would say to him:

" 'I understand you.' He would shrug his shoulders.

"Thus, with my vexation renewing itself daily, find-
ing myself more and more altered in my own eyes—
as in all eyes which might have cared to look at me,
had I not been condemned everlastingly to the oblivion
of all men!—I grew hungrier and hungrier for his
kindness. With his kisses and friendly embraces, it was
indeed a heaven, a gloomy heaven, which I entered,
and where I should have wished to be left, poor, deaf,
dumb, blind. Already I had the habit of it. I used to
see us as good children, free to walk in the Paradise
of sadness. We were in harmony with one another.
Much affected, we would work together. But after a
poignant caress, he would say: 'How funny it will seem
to you when I am no longer here, through whom you
have passed. When you no longer have my arms under
your neck, nor my heart to fall asleep on, nor this
mouth upon your eyes. For I shall have to go away,
very far, some day. Besides, I must help others; it is
my duty. Although this may not be at all appetizing
to you . . . dear soul.' All at once I foresaw myself,
with him gone, the prey of dizziness, plunged into the
most frightful shadow: death. I used to make him prom-

288

ise that he would not abandon me. He gave it twenty times, that lover's promise. It was as frivolous as my saying to him:

" 'I understand you.'

"Ah! I have never been jealous of him. He will not leave me, I think. What will happen? He has no connections; he will never do any work. He wants to live like a somnambulist. Will his kindness and charity alone give him rights in the world of the real? At times I forget the trouble into which I have fallen: he shall make me strong, we will travel, we will hunt in the deserts, we will sleep on the pavement of unknown cities, care-free, exempt from pain. Or I will wake up, and the laws and customs shall have changed,—thanks to his magic power; or the world, while remaining the same, shall leave me to my desires, pleasures, unconcerns. Oh! the life of adventure which exists in children's books, to comfort me for all I have suffered, will you give it me? He cannot. I am in the dark as to his ideal. He has told me that he has regrets, aspirations: that should not concern me. Does he talk to God? Perhaps I ought to appeal to God. I am at the very bottom of the abyss, and no longer know how to pray.

"If he were to explain his sorrows to me, should I understand them more than his mockeries? He attacks me, spends hours in making me ashamed of everything in the world which could have touched me, and becomes indignant if I weep.

" 'You see that polished young man, stepping into the beautiful calm house yonder: his name is Duval, Dufour, Armand, Maurice, I know not what? A woman has given her life up to loving the wicked idiot: she is dead, a saint in heaven certainly, at present. You would be the death of me, just as he was the death of that woman. It is our fate, we charitable hearts. . . .' Alas! there were days when the actions of all men made them seem to him the playthings of a grotesque delirium; he would laugh frightfully, for a long time.—Then, he would resume his ways of a young mother, of an elder sister. If he were less wild, we should be saved. But his tenderness also is deadly. I am subject to him.—Ah! I am foolish!

"One day, perhaps, he will vanish miraculously; but if he is to be taken up again into a heaven, I cannot fail to know, to look on in some measure at the assumption of my little friend!"

Peculiar household!

DELIRES II

ALCHEMY OF THE WORD

About me. Story of one of my follies.

For a long time I had boasted that I possessed all possible landscapes, and had laughed at the reputations of modern painting and poetry.

I was in love with crazy paintings, over-doors, decorations, tumbler's back-drops, signs, coloured prints; out of date literature, church Latin, lewd books without spelling, the novels of our ancestors, fairytales, little books for children, old librettos, silly refrains, naive rhythms.

290

I used to dream crusades, voyages of discovery of which we have no account, republics without a history, religious wars nipped in the bud, revolutions in custom, dislodgment of races and of continents: I believed in all the spells of magic.

I invented the colours of the vowels! . . . A black, E white, I red, O blue, U green.—I determined the form and movement of every consonant, and with the aid of instinctive rhythms, I flattered myself that I had invented a poetic language, which would one day or another be accessible to all the senses. I reserved the right of translation.

At first it was a sort of research. I would write silences, nights; I noted the inexpressible. I used to fixate vertigoes.

Loin des oiseaux, des troupeaux, des villageoises,
Que buvais-je, à genoux dans cette bruyère
Entourée de tendres bois de noisetiers,
Dans un brouillard d'après-midi tiède et vert?
Que pouvais-je boire dans cette jeune Oise,
—Ormeaux sans voix, gazon sans fleurs, ciel couvert!—
Boire à ces gourdes jaunes, loin de ma case
Chérie? Quelque liqueur d'or qui fait suer.

Je faisais une louche enseigne d'auberge.
—Un orage vint chasser le ciel. Au soir
L'eau des bois se perdait sur les sables vierges,
Le vent de Dieu jetait des glaçons aux mares;
Pleurant, je voyais de l'or,—et ne pus boire.—

À quatre heures du matin, l'été,
Le sommeil d'amour dure encore.
Sous les bocages s'évapore
  L'odeur de soir fêté.

Là-bas, dans leur vaste chantier,
Au soleil des Hespérides,
Déjà s'agitent—en bras de chemise—
   Les Charpentiers.

Dans leurs Déserts de mousse, tranquilles,
Ils préparent les lambris précieux
     Où la ville
   Peindra de faux cieux.

O, pour ces Ouvriers, charmants
Sujets d'un roi de Babylone,
Vénus! quitte un instant les Amants
   Dont l'âme est en couronne!

   O Reine des Bergers,
Porte aux travailleurs l'eau-de-vie
Que leurs forces soient en paix
   En attendant le bain dans la mer à midi.

The old tricks of poetry played an important part in my alchemy of the Word.

I accustomed myself to plain hallucination: quite frankly I used to see a mosque in place of a factory, a school of drums made by angels, carriages on the roads of heaven, a parlour at the bottom of a lake, monsters, mysteries; a ballad title raised up terrors before me.

Then I explained my magical sophistries with the hallucination of words!

I ended by deeming holy the confusion of my mind. I was lazy, prey to a sluggish fever: I envied animals their contentment,—caterpillars which symbolize the innocence of limbo, moles, the sleep of virginity.

My nature became embittered. I said good-bye to the world in kinds of romances:

CHANSON DE LA PLUS HAUTE TOUR

Qu'il vienne, qu'il vienne,
Le temps dont on s'éprenne.

J'ai tant fait patience
Qu'à jamais j'oublie.
Craintes et souffrances
Aux cieux sont parties.
Et la soif malsaine
Obscurcit mes veines.

Qu'il vienne, qu'il vienne,
Le temps dont on s'éprenne.

Telle la prairie
A l'oubli livrée
Grandie, et fleurie
D'encens et d'ivraies,
Au bourdon farouche
De très sales mouches

Qu'il vienne, qu'il vienne,
Le temps dont on s'éprenne.

I was fond of desert land, burnt orchards, shop-worn merchandise, tepid drinks. I dragged myself through stinking alleys, and with eyes shut, offered myself to the sun, the fire god.

"General, if there is still an old cannon left on your ramparts in ruins, bombard us with dried blocks of earth. Before the mirrors of the splendid shops! In the salons! Make the town eat its dust. Oxidize the gargoyles. Fill the boudoirs with the burning powder of rubies. . . ."

Oh! the little fly drunk at the tavern urinal, amorous of borage, and which a ray of light dissolves!

FAIM

Si j'ai du goût, ce n'est guère
Que pour la terre et les pierres.
Je déjeune toujours d'air,
De roc, de charbons, de fer.

Mes faims, tournez. Paissez, faims,
  Le pré des sons.
Attirez le gai venin
  Des liserons.

Mangez les cailloux qu'on brise,
Les vieilles pierres d'églises;
Les galets des vieux déluges,
Pains semés dans les vallées grises.

Le loup criait sous les feuilles
En crachant les belles plumes
De son repas de volailles:
Comme lui je me consume.

  Les salades, les fruits
N'attendent que la cueillette;
Mais l'araignée de la haie
Ne mange que des violettes.

Que je dorme! que je bouille
    Aux autels de Salomon.
Le bouillon court sur la rouille,
    Et se mêle au Cédron.

At length, O happiness, O reason, I stripped away the sky's azure, which is blackness, and lived, gold spark of the radiance *nature*. From joy I began to wear an expression of comic and complete derangement.

Elle est retrouvée!
Quoi? l'Éternité.
C'est la mer mêlée
    Au soleil.

Mon âme éternelle,
Observe ton voeu
Malgré la nuit seule
Et le jour en feu.

Donc tu te dégages
Des humains suffrages,
Des communs élans!
Tu voles selon. . . .

Jamais l'espérance,
    Pas *d'orietur*.
Science et patience,
Le supplice est sûr.

Plus de lendemain
Braises de satin
Votre ardeur
Est le devoir.

Elle est retrouvée !
—Quoi ?—l'Éternité.
C'est la mer mêlée
Au soleil.

I became a fabulous opera: I saw that all creatures have a fatality for happiness: action is not life, but a way of spoiling some power, an enervation. Morality is softening of the brain.

Every creature seemed to me to be endowed with several *other* lives. This gentleman does not know what he is doing: he is an angel. This family is a litter of puppies. Before a number of men I would talk aloud with a moment of one of their other existences.—In this way I loved a pig.

Not one of the sophistries of madness,—that madness which one shuts up inside oneself,—have I forgot: I could repeat them all, I remember the system.

My health was endangered. Fear came. I used to fall into periods of sleep lasting for several days, from which I got up again only to resume the most depressing reveries. I was ripe for death, and by a dangerous route my weakness brought me to the confines of Cimmeria, the land of shadow and whirlwinds.

I had to travel, to seek distraction from the spells that were gathered in my head. On the sea which I loved as though it were to wash me clean of defilement, I watched the dawn of the consoling cross. I had been damned by the rainbow. Happiness was my doom, my remorse, my worm: my life must always be too vast to be given up to strength and beauty.

Happiness! Her tooth, sweet unto death, used to

warn me at cock-crow,—*ad matutinum*, at the *Christus venit*,—in the gloomiest towns:

> O saisons, ô châteaux!
> Quelle âme est dans défauts!
>
> J'ai fait la magique étude
> Du bonheur, qu'aucun n'élude.
>
> Salut à lui chaque fois
> Que chante le coq gaulois.
>
> Ah! je n'aurai plus d'envie:
> Il s'est chargé de ma vie.
>
> Ce charme a pris âme et corps
> Et dispersé les efforts.
>
> O saisons, ô châteaux!
>
> L'heure de la fuite, hélas!
> Sera l'heure du trépas.
>
> O saisons, ô châteaux!

That is over. To-day I know how to honour beauty.

THE IMPOSSIBLE

Ah! that life of my childhood, the highroad in all weathers, preternaturally solemn, more disinterested than the best of beggars, proud to have neither country nor friends; what nonsense it was.—And I see it only now.

297

I was right in despising these good fellows who lose no opportunity for a caress, parasites of the cleanliness and health of our women, nowadays, when they are at such cross purposes with us.

I have been right in all my scorns: because I am running away!

Running away?

I explain.

Only yesterday I was sighing: "Heavens! are there not enough of us damned down here! I myself have been so long already in their company. I know them all. We always recognize one another; we sicken one another. Charity is unknown to us. But we are civil; our relations with society are very respectable." Is it surprising? The world! business men, simple fellows!—We are not looked down on. But the elect, how would they receive us? Now there are surly and joyous persons, not the true elect, since one needs audacity or humility if one is to approach them. They are the only elect. They utter no blessings.

Finding that I have still two pennies of common sense,—that is quickly spent!—I see that my unhappiness comes from not having realized soon enough that we are in the Occident. The Occidental swamps! Not that I believe the light altered, form shrunken, movement gone astray. . . . Good! right here my spirit desires absolutely to take upon itself all the cruel developments the spirit has undergone since the end of the Orient. . . . It desires this, does my spirit!

My two pennies of common sense are spent! The spirit is authority. It wants me to be in the Occident. I should have to make it be silent in order to conclude as I should like to.

Crowns of martyrdom, triumphs of art, pride of inventors, ardour of pirates—bade them all go to the devil. I returned to the East and to the ancient and eternal wisdom.—It seems that this is a dream of gross indolence!

Yet, I was not thinking particularly of the pleasure of escaping from modern sufferings. I had not in mind the bastard wisdom of the Koran.—But is it not a real affliction, that ever since that declaration of science, Christianity, man has been *playing*, proving his evidence, satiating himself with the pleasure of repeating those proofs, and living only in that way? Subtle, ridiculous torture; source of my spiritual aberrations. Nature can grow bored, perhaps! M. Prudhomme was born with Christ.

It is not because we cultivate fog? We eat fever with our watery vegetables. And drunkenness! and tobacco! and ignorance! and devotions!—Is all that far enough from the thought of the wisdom of the East, the first country? Why a modern world at all, if such poisons are invented!

The churchmen will say: We understand. But you are talking about the Garden of Eden. Nothing for you in the history of the Oriental peoples.—True; it is of Eden that I was dreaming! What has the purity of ancient races to do with my dreams?

The philosophers: The world has no age. Humanity simply shifts from place to place. You happen to be in the Occident, but you are free to live in your Orient,

299

as old a one as you please,—and to live there comfortably. Don't be a victim. Philosophers, you belong to your Occident.

My spirit, be wary. No violent taking sides to win salvation. Exert yourself!—Ah! science does not move fast enough for us!—But I perceive that my spirit is asleep.

If it were always wide awake from this moment on, we should soon have arrived at the truth, which perhaps surrounds us with its weeping angels! . . . If it had been awake up to now, I should not then have yielded to harmful instincts at an immemorial epoch! . . . If it had always been wide awake, I should be sailing in full wisdom! . . .

O purity! purity!

It is this minute of wakefulness that has given me the vision of purity!—By the spirit one goes to God!

Heart-rending misfortune!

THE LIGHTNING

Human toil! that is the explosion which from time to time lights up my abyss.

"Nothing is vanity; science and forward!" cries the modern Ecclesiastes, which is to say *everybody*. And yet the carcasses of the wicked and of the slothful fall upon the hearts of the rest. . . . Ah! hurry, hurry a little; out there, beyond the night, those rewards, future, everlasting . . . shall we miss them? . . .

What can I do? I know toil of old; and science is too slow. Let prayer gallop and let the light roar. . . .

I see perfectly. It is too easy, and the weather is too warm; they get on without me. I have my duty; I will show my pride in it, after the manner of some others, by setting it aside.

My life is worn out. Let us make believe, let us idle away, O pity! And we will live for our own amusement, dreaming monstrous loves, and fantastic universes, complaining and finding fault with the lineaments of the world, acrobat, beggar, artist, bandit,—priest! On my bed in the hospital, the smell of incense has come back to me so overpoweringly: keeper of the holy perfumes, confessor, martyr. . . .

There I recognize the vile education of my childhood. What then! . . . Go my twenty years if others go twenty. . . .

No! no! at present I rebel against death! Work seems too easy for my pride; my betrayal to the world would be too brief a penalty. At the last moment I should strike out right and left. . . .

Then,—Oh!—dear, poor soul, would eternity not be lost to us!

MORNING

Had I not *once* an amiable, heroic, fabulous youth, to write on leaves of gold, "too much luck!" Through what crime, through what error, have I earned my present weakness? You who maintain that animals groan with vexation, that sick men despair, that the dead dream ill, try to tell the story of my fall and of my sleep. I myself can no more explain than the beggar

301

with his continual *Paters* and *Ave Marias. I no longer know how to talk!*

Yet I believe that to-day I have finished the tale of my hell. It was hell, certainly; the ancient one, whose gates the Son of Man opened.

From the same desert, out of the same night, always my tired eyes woke to the silver star, always, while the Kings of life, the three Magi, heart, soul and mind, did not stir! When shall we go out beyond shores and mountains, to greet the birth of the new toil, of the new wisdom, the flight of tyrants and demons, the end of superstition; to adore,—the first!—Christmas on earth?

The song of the skies, the march of peoples! Slaves, let us not slander life.

ADIEU

Autumn already!—But why long for a sun that will last forever, when we are busy with the discovery of the divine light,—far from the men who die on the seasons?

Autumn. My bark, whose sails were set in the move-less fog, turns toward the port of misery, the immense city with skies stained by fire and mud. Ah! the rotten rags, the bread soaked with rain, the drunkenness, the thousand loves which crucified me. She will have no end, then, that ghoulish queen of a million souls and bodies, which are dead *and which will be judged!* I see myself again, my skin eaten by mire and plague, my hair, my armpits full of worms, and still bigger

302

worms in my heart, stretched among unknown men, age-less, feelingless . . . I might have died there . . . Frightful evocation! I abhor squalor!

And I am afraid of winter because it is the season of comfort!—Sometimes in the sky I see infinite strands covered with white nations in joy. Above me, a great ship of gold flutters its many-coloured pennons in the morning wind. I have created all pageants, all tri-umphs, all dramas. I have attempted the invention of new flowers, new stars, new flesh, new tongues. I have believed myself the possessor of supernatural powers. Well! I am going to bury my imagination and my memories! A fine artist's and story-teller's reputation gone to the devil!

I! I who called myself a wizard or an angel, free from every rule of morality, am brought back to earth with a job to look out for and harsh reality to embrace! Peasant!

Am I mistaken? would charity be death's sister to me?

Finally I will ask forgiveness for having fed myself on lies, and I am off.

But not one friendly hand! and where shall I ask for help?

Yes, this new hour is at worst very hard.

For I can say that victory is mine: the teeth-gritting, fire-breathing and pestilential gasps abate. All mem-ories of the world are fading. My last regrets are with-drawn,—envy of beggars, thieves, friends of death, hangers-back of all sorts.—You damned ones, if I were to avenge myself!

It is necessary to be absolutely modern.

No canticles: hold to the step you have gained. Sore night! The dried blood smokes on my face, and I have nothing at my back but this horrible bush! . . . The battle of the spirit is as brutal as the clash of men; but the perception of justice is the pleasure of God alone.

This, however, is the vigil. Welcome every influx of true vigour and tenderness. And at dawn, armed with eager patience, we will enter the splendid towns.

What was I saying about a friendly hand! One advantage is that I can laugh at the old, false passions, and put to shame those lying couples,—I have seen the hell of women down there;—and it will be legitimate for me to *possess the truth in a soul and body*.

April-August, 1873.

Translated by J. S. Watson, Jr.

THE DRUNKEN BOAT

As I slid down the impassible river narrows,
I felt no longer guided by the bargemen;
From painted stakes they hung, shot through with
    arrows,
Squalling redskins had taken them for targets.

I did not wait for baggage to embark,
For bearers of British cotton, Flemish stone,
But when my guides lay scalpless in the dark,
The rivers and my will remained, alone.

Muffled as a child in the womb's mesh,
I ran, last winter, in the sea's surf-merriment,
Envy the water's welcome of my flesh,
Peninsulas cracked off by continents!

Kind storms poured out their mischief on my head,
Without the ninny eyes of lantern guides,
Over eternal dungeons of the dead,
Lighter than a cork, I danced the tides.

Tender as flesh of apples to a child,
With stains of blue wine, vomitings, and film,

Up through my shell came the green water wild,
And laved me, splitting grappling hook and helm.

And I have since bathed in the milk and swale
Of the poem sea, infused with stars around,
Devoured its glaucous depths where sometimes floats the
     pale,
Rapt, brooding body of a man who is drowned.

Where dyeing the deep with deliriums and fires,
And tender rhythms, under day's rutilant roof,
Stronger than whiskey, vaster than your lyres,
Ferments the bitter rust-red froth of love!

I know skies scratched with lightning, waterspouts,
The surf, the current, the evening near to me,
The dawn exalted as a flight of doves,
And I have seen what men believe to see.

I saw the low sun spotted like a snake
Illumine violet curds, and the waves, and the breeze,
Like antique actors with a play to make,
Raise up the trembling blooms of anemones.

I dreamed of dazzling snows upon the laps
Of green nights, and kisses an outcast ocean heard,
The circulation of unforgettable saps,
The blue and yellow cries of phosphorus birds,

For months I followed the hysterical hooves
Of rabid waves in their mad rockward beat,
Nor dreamed the muzzle for those snorting droves
Was lifted by the Virgin's luminous feet.
306

I touched, do you hear? on Floridas that sang,
Heaped high with flowers and skins of men and eyes
Of panthers, where the burnished rainbows hang
Like reins of green sea sheep, from copper skies.

Fermenting fens, enormous nets, where stirs
Leviathan rotting in a reedy rout;
And waters raving round the calmest waters,
And black gulfs putting the horizons out!

Glaciers, silver suns, pearl waves and enrous skies,
And hideous valleys yellow with disease
Where giant serpents eaten away by flies
Fall with black perfumes from contorted trees!

I would have shown to children these doradoes
Of the blue wave, the golden fish, that sings.
The foam of flowers has blessed my voyaging,
And winds ineffable have lent me wings.

At times a martyr weary of zones and poles,
The sea whose sobbing made my buffets dear,
Showed me shadow flowers in yellow shoals,
Sweeter than a woman, lying near,

Until an island tossed about my side
The quarrels and dung of blond-eyed birds that weep,
And I sailed until across my fragile lines
The bodies of the drowned came down to sleep. . . .

Then I, boat lost beneath the hair of rivers,
Flung by the tempest into birdless ether,
I whom no Monitors, no Hansa schooners
Could have fished up, a carcass drunk with water,

Free, fuming, risen from the purple's heart,
Who bored the sky, a ruddy wall that keeps
For all good poets exquisite jelly tarts,
Moss of the sunlight, dribblings of the deep.

Who running spotted with electric rings,
Black hippocampi answering my cry,
When the blue skies were battered, bleeding things
Under the bludgeonings of red July,

Who trembled hearing fifty leagues away
Behemoth rutting, groan, and Maelstrom's grind,
Eternal spinner of blue peace at play,
I long for Europe, antique, turret-lined.

I saw star-archipelagoes! Islands of delight
Whose delirious skies lie open to the wanderer:
Sleep you self-exiled in unbottomed night,
O countless golden birds, O future Vigor?

But I have wept too much, Dawn breaks the heart,
  there seems
Vileness in moonlight, in the sun, to me.
Harsh love has stuffed me like a bag with dreams.
Oh! let my keel burst! Let me go to the sea!

I want none of Europe's waters unless it be the pale
Cold murky puddle with the twilight nigh
Where a child may sit with sadness, and let sail
A boat as frail as a May butterfly.

I can no longer, bathing in your swoons,
O waves, raise up their wash to dirty dredgers,
Nor cross the pride of flags, the flame of noons,
Nor swim beneath the horrible eyes of barges!

(Translated by Lionel Abel)

VOWEL SONNET

A black, E white, I red, U green, O blue,
Vowels; some day I shall reveal your birth:
A, black velvet swarm of flies that over earth
Buzz to the foulest stench, abyss of hue
Sombre; E frank with smoke and fierce intents,
Spears of proud glaciers, white kings, blossom-lips;
I purple of spitting blood, laugh of fair lips
In anger or in drunken penitence;
U cycles, divine rhythm of the seas,
Peace of beast-strewn pastures, of wrinkles that crease
Brows whereon the furrow of learning lies;
O, great lightning, with strange clamors hurled
Over the quiet of angels and the world,
O omega, violet ray of her eyes.

Translated by Joseph T. Shipley

THE SEEKERS OF LICE

When, forehead full of torments hot and red,
    The child invokes white clouds of hazy dreams,
Two sisters tall and sweet draw near his bed,
    Whose fingers frail nails tip with silvery gleams.

The child before a window open wide,
    Where blue air bathes a maze of flowers, they sit;
And in his heavy hair dew falls, while glide
    Their fingers terrible with charm through it.

Rich as from roses swung amid wet leaves,
    Their furtive breathing croons or is disturbed
By a salival lisp, while the lip retrieves
    Some deep desire to kiss a qualm has curbed.

Through perfumed silences their sable lashes
    Beat slow; he hears in colourless dim drowse,
How, trapped by soft electric fingers, smashes
    Between tyrannic nails each tiny louse.

Then wells in him the wine of idleness,
    Delirious power, the harmonica's soft sigh:
The child still feels to their long drawn caress
    Ceaselessly heave and swoon a wish to cry.

Translated by T. Sturge Moore